...LSH TALES

Curious Welsh Tales

Geraint Roberts

First published – 2023

© Text: Geraint Roberts

ISBN 978-1-84524-513-9

Cover design: Eirian Evans

Front cover photos: Cwmorthin Chapel – Chapter 10
The Weight Lifting Stone – Chapter 18

Back cover photos: Sian Groca's Stone – Chapter 12
The Devil's Thumb – Chapter 13
The Forbidden Beach – Chapter 4

Published by Gwasg Carreg Gwalch,
12 Iard yr orsaf, Llanrwst, Wales LL26 0EH
☎ 01492 642031
email: books@carreg-gwalch.cymru
website: www.carreg-gwalch.cymru

Printed and published in Wales

I would like to dedicate this book to my children, Dylan, Eifion, Megan and Robert who endured/enjoyed their share of being exposed to "my interesting places with stories."

Contents

About the Author

Having had a childhood brought up in the countryside of North and Mid Wales playing and being outdoors it was perhaps natural that the author became very much a country boy.

He then spent his first ten years' working life as an Outdoor Education Instructor, mainly in Eryri when he consolidated both this love for the outdoors as well as the rich history and colourful legends steeped in the area, an interest which was first instilled into him by his father.

Throughout his adulthood all aspects of outside activities continued to play an important role in his life with such diverse disciplines as fell-running, walking, caving, cycling, kayaking and sailing. Many of these activities took him to secluded, out of the way places and he soon realized no matter how remote a location was, there would always be something interesting to be discovered. This curiosity became his philosophy and often led to some obsessive research which invariably meant a return visit.

A venue becomes more than a nice place when the historical significance of a particular boulder hiding in the gorse is known, a legend surrounding an ancient bridge is told, the story about who once lived in an old abandoned ruin is related or who sought refuge in a hidden cave.

Told to generations of children, including of course his own; outdoor Wales was made to come alive and adventurous rambles through pleasant countryside became something much more.

Some of these old stories, told by word of mouth are on the point of being forgotten and lost forever, one only has to peruse our OS maps to see so many provocatively colourful place names whose explanations have been lost in the mist of time. He spent the last fifteen years of his career as Head of a primary school before retiring in 2010 to spend his time cycling, bowling and researching more such tales; ... which he can write about.

Acknowledgements

I would like to acknowledge the kind permission granted by the following for photographs used in the book:-

Dudley Caving Club
San Ffagan Folk Museum
Brecon Museum

I would also like to offer my gratitude to the following people, they will know why they are being thanked.

Ashley O'Dwyer, Gwynfryn Williams, (Binks), Dafydd Roberts, Gareth Griffiths, Owen Jones (my uncle Now) Dai, Steve, Hazel Griffiths, Meira Lloyd, Pete Jones, Donald, Rees, Jan Roberts, Jonathan Jones, Anette Connah, Margaret Roberts, Megan and Owain Bevan, Richard Huws, Gwenllian Aubrey, Angharad Fychan, Philip Jones, Jackie Morgan and a one time acquaintance who sported a beard, wore a cravat and smoked a pipe! I offer the usual caveat apologising to anyone I may have inadvertently omitted from this list.

I am reserving a very special thank you to Cledwyn Fychan whose selfless leads, inspiration, proof reading and kind comments played a significant part in the writing of this book. Diolch yn fawr Cledwyn.

Foreward

Geraint Roberts could never be content to just read or hear an old story. No, he would have to dig down into the very roots and then go and see where the story took place for himself.

Each journey might begin in the archival world of Tithe maps, old documents, books from his own considerable library or obscure old magazines.

He would then progress to finding 'local characters' who might have their own handed down oral versions of what really happened. The journey might then continue into the bowels of the earth, crawling along fragile underground tunnels or kayaking through the treacherous tidal currents swirling around our rocky shores. He has walked and cycled through bogs and over mountains, climbed rocks and navigated through thick forests all over Wales to get to, and always with his camera the very nests whence these stories hatched.

He playfully describes many of his own adventures in an eloquent, laid back style of writing impregnated with his own brand of subtle humour. It is obvious the little boy is still in him.

No one could read this book without wanting to go and seek at least some of the locations described.

Cledwyn Fychan

Introduction

If you've enjoyed reading my book it may well be that you are now reading this Introduction, it seems that's what most people do.

Many of these stories have appeared as articles in various magazines and papers in both English and Welsh over the years and have ended up as chapters in this book because several people have suggested the idea.

I have been deliberately vague about the precise locations described in these anecdotes. If you really want to go and seek these interesting places for yourself, the process of finding their exact whereabouts will add to the enjoyment; it certainly did for me.

Some of them are really difficult to get to and you might consider that reading about them with a liberal dose of imagination will suffice.

Most of the photos are ones I have taken with a variety of cameras over the years. Some of them are poor quality but have been included because they were taken at the time of the related story. The other photos have been duly acknowledged.

Any errors, factual or otherwise can be laid squarely on my doorstep.

I must admit to have struggled with a title for this book because what you have in-between these covers is a varied compilation of history, folklore, and accounts of my own personal experiences; several of them forming the very essence of these stories.

Although the book includes stories from all over Wales it is perhaps forgivable that the bulk of the chapters describe tales which occurred in Northern and Central Wales which has been my stamping ground for so many years.

If you're reading this introduction before you read the book, then please – enjoy it!

Chapter 1

Glyndŵr's Cave?

If there is a cave in Wales which hasn't got a legend I would be surprised, most claim to have played host to someone of note with an accompanying story. Indeed, finding the story is the easy part, finding the cave is usually harder. In this first chapter I describe a walk I made in Snowdonia looking for one cave but finding five.

Ogof Elen Luyddog

Hafod Garegog

Imagine, two old friends sharing a skein of mead and putting the world as they knew it to rights. It is 1412 and the host, Rhys Goch is entertaining the erstwhile Chieftain of the Dee valley, and almost Prince of free Wales, Owain Glyndŵr. They are in Hafod Garegog close to the Glaslyn estuary which in those pre Porthmadog embankment days brought high tides to within two miles of Beddgelert. Glyndŵr's bid for an independent Wales is on the wane, his early momentum lost and he has come to his old friend to seek some breathing space and temporary refuge. Hafod Garegog even today is deep in a remote wooded valley, tranquil and beautiful and surrounded in verdant growth. A perfect haven to seek safety.

However, it isn't to be. A servant rushes in with word of soldiers approaching, Glyndŵr must flee! He seizes his companion's arm, they exchange a few words and quickly embrace, then with literally minutes to spare he hastily rushes out of the house and heads north west towards the estuary.

Glyndŵr's bid for Welsh independence had actually started as a local dispute with Lord Grey of Dyffryn Clwyd which escalated into a bigger and nobler cause. Grey seemingly had the king's ears and Glyndŵr's case was not fairly dealt with.

Early successes and captured castles were further buoyed

by setting up a Welsh Parliament in Machynlleth in 1404. He even forged an alliance with the French and the two armies marched against Henry IV at Worcester in 1405 only for both sides to tactically withdraw following a bizarre three day stand-off which comprised of several single combats, but little else.

By 1409 he had lost his last stronghold and was reduced to conducting a slowly diminishing guerilla campaign, and was last seen by his enemies in 1412.

Generations of embellished and imagined legends honed in their telling will describe his swim across the Glaslyn to reach the southern slopes of Moel Hebog where he will have to climb for his life.

Heading up the complicated slopes of rocks, heather and bracken, fuelled by fear and adrenalin he soon reaches Bryn Bannog, the main shoulder of Moel Hebog mountain. A small squad of soldiers are still pursuing him, mere minutes away. Should he traverse right and aim for the fastness of Snowdonia or turn left for the wooded valley of Cwm Pennant?

He chose to continue up the steepening ridge to his right breathlessly forcing each leg forward, his eyes constantly scanning ahead for the easiest route; within the hour he was to rue that decision. If he could only reach the eastern flank of Hebog he could drop down to the valley and gain the lower slopes of Snowdon itself where he would be safe.

He gained the upper reaches of Cwm Cyd and was just starting downhill when he saw some movement and the glint of metal two hundred yards below. It was another band of soldiers coming up from the direction of Beddgelert to cut him off. He was trapped! Death was snapping at his heels, and the same fate was rapidly coming to meet him; rearing up on his left were the awesome north facing cliffs of Moel Hebog closing around him in a huge semi circle.

In desperation he made for the only weakness visible in the cliff face, a steep gully, and with the English soldiers closing in he began to climb. Several times he almost slipped, a few loose holds came off and more than once he thought he couldn't go any further. Today, by modern standards the climb is considered easy but clad in leather boots with crossbow bolts pinging off the rock past his ears and angry curses following his every move it must have been harrowing. None dared follow him, a soldier's pay didn't cover that sort of risk! Glyndŵr however had no choice! Eventually he climbed out of sight as the steepness of the cliff face relented. He scrambled to easier ground and headed off along the summit ridge to safety. It had been a close shave.

Modern climbing guidebooks amusingly credit Owain Glyndwr as having made the first ascent of 'Y Simdde' (The Chimney).

He was to spend the next few days hiding in a cave nearby. This is where this chapter of his story ends and mine begins; when I decided to go and look for the cave.

It was a frosty February morning when I parked the car in Beddgelert Forest campsite refreshingly empty of its normal

Distant view of Ogof Elen Luyddog

summer clientele elbowing for the best pitches. I followed a footpath diligently clinging to the Meillionen stream with signposts every so often to "Glyndŵr's Cave" – how convenient!

The walk up was beautiful as the sun's rays occasionally broke through the fir canopy to highlight small glades of moss and ferns whose ecosystems had evolved around a fallen tree or a large boulder. Small triangles of ice adorned the laughing brook at its edges like the skin of a milky coffee, only as bright as crystal where they were caressed by the sun. I crossed the odd forest track always with a "Glyndŵr's Cave" sign as the path continued to climb beside the stream. The forest ended at a boundary fence and the Meillionen became a series of gurgling ditches losing themselves in the rapidly steepening slope. The final sign stood there slightly tilted and embarrassingly vague! Four hundred steep feet higher one could just about discern a small cave at the base of a gully cleaving a forbidding buttress of rock which seemed to scowl on the whole valley.

This was the Glyndŵr cave the forestry was presenting to the public without actually saying so; and there was a good reason for this.

Having done some research before embarking on my 'cave quest' I had learnt that the cave I could see from the edge of the forest was actually one of only a handful of disused asbestos mines in northern Wales, the others being on Anglesey. The cave I was looking for was above and to the right of the gully, on the actual face of the scowling buttress and was a dangerous place to reach. It was also known as Ogof Elen Luyddog, a folk memory reference to Helen, wife of the Roman ruler Macsen.

Twenty sweaty minutes later I stepped into the cheerless mine whose sloping floor went in about twenty feet and whilst I was was inspecting the white fibrous vein oozing out of the wall I pondered on the little story I'd heard about the Trwyn y Gader mine on Anglesey. A handkerchief made of the asbestos had apparently been presented to George III. I tried to imagine

Gwylfa Glyndŵr, his observation cleft.

the response such a gift would receive from Buckingham Palace today! Long before asbestos dust was known to be dangerous the romans used it to make cremation shrouds for their most prominent citizens. This ensured that the ash taken away for whatever ritualistic ceremony they had in mind was not tainted by any wood ash.

The approach to Ogof Elen was up an easy but exposed gully on the very flank of the steep cliff, I then had to carefully balance along a ledge with a sheer drop of two hundred feet mere inches away! Any wind would have made it tricky! No wonder the forestry commission were content to leave their last 'Glyndŵr's Cave' sign far enough away to ambiguously suggest it to be the far safer asbestos mine! The cave was shallow and would have provided shelter from anywhere but weather from the east. It only had one approach, an ideal place to defend if you were a goat keeping wolves at bay, but useless for anything more than a single night for a Welsh hero. I descended the Tolkien like scramble and took my bearings for the next candidate I had short listed as Glyndŵr's cave.

Another possibility which had been mooted lay in the rough scree below the scowling cliff. An accidental settling of one rock on another was an unlikely choice for shelter longer than a passing rain shower and I quickly dismissed it.

A Showell Styles article from the 1970s offered two alternatives in the next cwm to the east. These were over a rocky ridge rising out of the upper reaches of the forest and would take some finding. Getting there wasn't going to be easy either. I would have to climb back down to the forestry and traverse across hoping a track or fire break would take me

The best candidate for Ogof Glyndwr

through the dense conifers. Then I would have to scramble up on to the rocky ridge before dropping down into the next shallow cwm to begin my search. It is usually easier finding a rock or a cave from below. As I passed the last 'Glyndŵr's Cave' sign on my way down I allowed myself a wry smile as I wondered how many campers over the years had congratulated themselves for having visited Glyndŵr's Cave on their way down from the old mine!

Forty minutes later and I was looking for a way down off the rocky ridge. Every rock and shadow vied to become a possible cave and it became energy sapping work on the steep wet ground, many of the shadows still retaining last night's frost as I clambered around in the heather investigating every mini craglet.

Suddenly I saw it! I had found what had been described as Glyndŵr's observation cleft; it was certainly an impressive piece of glacial architecture. Perched high on the shoulder of

Asbestos Mine

the rocky ridge it had to be stumbled upon. A huge vertical crack with a side entry provided excellent views all the way down the slope to the valley; it was a good hiding place but having no roof had limited value as an abode. According to Styles another more suitable cave lay a few hundred feet below near what had become known as Glyndŵr's well.

This took some finding. A chance leaning of one huge slab of rock on another was well hidden amongst a small boulder field. It would have been easy to miss. Inside was dry and relatively flat with the floor space perhaps of a three seater sofa. And although there was no room to stand, some dry rushes, bracken and heather would make a comfortable shelter and keep the elements out. It was very well camouflaged and this could have been improved with more rocks and heather. Thirty yards away a small spring bubbled beneath a veneer of ice confirming this cave to be the best candidate of the day.

Incidents which happened centuries ago, whose details are only recorded as legends will only ever stay as legends, we must accept that. But the very vagueness offers the licence to speculate within an acceptable balance of probability. It is highly likely that he would have sought safety in Snowdonia and it is highly possible that generations of story telling placing him on these slopes are true; is there smoke without fire? Between them, Rhys Goch and the Abbot of Beddgelert are said to have kept him supplied with food for the duration of his sojourn on Moel Hebog.

I took a drink from his well and briefly reflected on his story. Very soon after this climbing and cave chapter in the twilight of his career he vanished into history to perpetuate another myth that he, like King Arthur would somehow return when Wales most needed him. He refused a pardon and despite a reward for his capture he was never betrayed. It is thought he ended his days living with his daughter Alys near Hereford. There is a portrait of one Sion Cent said to be Glyndŵr incognito, who can tell? He was an enigma to the end. I wondered about the thoughts which went through his head as he supped water from this very well as the sun sank behind the mountain in the evenings. He may have lain on his rough bedding re-living his famous victory at Hyddgen in 1401 when his 500 troops, surrounded and outnumbered by 1500 Flemish mercenaries had done the unexpected and charged to rout the fleeing army, leaving 200 dead. The site is still marked by two quartz boulders, the 'Covenant Stones'. Did he I wonder, regret failing to support Hotspur in 1403 at the battle of Shrewsbury where his additional troops might very well have changed the course of history?

Or did he reflect on the words of a monk he had hailed one morning commenting how early he had risen? The monk replied "Not as early as you my Lord, you have risen a century too early!"

Chapter 2

The Lost Lake

This episode illustrates what happened when I followed up on a story read from a dusty old book I bought from a dusty old second hand bookshop.

Craig y Llam

A little over thirty years ago whilst researching for my book 'The Lakes of Eryri' (this isn't a plug by the way because unfortunately the book is now out of print!) I came across a reference to a lake which seemingly, didn't exist. It had so many snippets of interesting information though that I decided to not only include it in the book but to go and look for its site and its associated story.

An early 1919 OS map clearly showed where Llyn y Tri Greyenyn used to be; almost at the top of the Tal-y-llyn Pass, by the side of the A487. It had five other names, Llyn Bach (Little lake), Llyn Bwlch (Lake of the Col), Llyn Pen Morfa (Lake above the Fen), Llyn Bisodd y Gawres (Lake formed by the giantess's pee) and the Three Pebble Pool which is the English translation of its main name. The pebbles are three huge boulders which the giant Idris stopped to remove from his sandals one evening on his way to the summit of the mountain bearing his name – Cadair Idris. Here, unless folk memory has confused him with someone else he would spend the night stargazing. I would assume the giantess who was caught short and formed the lake was either his sister or his wife. This particular name for the lake appeared on War Office maps issued for the area during the second global conflict.

Above the lake a steep dark cliff rears up out of the scree with the sinister names of Craig y Llam (Cliff of the Leap); and Llam y lladron (Robber's leap) with good reason. Apparently it was here that local wrong doers were brought many years ago if found guilty, to be thrown over the edge to their deaths. Sheep rustlers were apparently blindfolded and spun around. If they walked over the edge they were obviously guilty but if they walked away from the cliff it was a sign of their innocence! Executions in those days were meant to be entertaining!

On one particular occasion however the purveyors of justice received more entertainment than they had expected. The condemned man asked to shake the hand of the judge because he felt that he had received a fair trial despite the outcome. No doubt flattered, the judge agreed and the very instant their hands clasped the man gave an ear piercing scream and leaped over the edge taking the judge with him!

Early travellers could discern the shapes of a priest and a bellringer high in the composition of the rocks. In keeping with the rather sinister connotation of name giving, an obvious mini tower known as the Devil's Pulpit can be seen overlooking the road some four hundred yards lower down the valley.

These days the summit of the cliff which can be reached from the other side on a minor road is a favourite spot to watch low flying jets, thankfully, slightly more innocuous entertainment!

Folklore had the dark peaty water of Llyn y Tri Greyenyn as bottomless and even when a bullock being driven from Dolgellau market in the early years of last century ran off the road and waded across barely wetting its belly the little lake's bottomless reputation remained intact!

Another tale is told of a gypsy caravan being towed by a couple of horses in a terrific thunderstorm. As they reached the side of the lake a lightning strike frightened the horses causing them to bolt. The caravan overturned fatally injuring them both and they had to be put down. The rushes at the spot where they are buried has always been a slightly different shade of green.

The summer of 1921 was particularly dry and the little lake only just survived. Then, during the

Devil's Pulpit

Ty'n y Gornel hotel

winter of 1925 a huge rockfall occurred partly filling the western shore. No sooner had this happened a road widening scheme further disrupted the little lake's recovery and by summer's end in 1926 Llyn y Tri Greyenyn had ceased to exist.

Away down the valley to the west another more significant lake which occupies the valley floor presents a photogenic canvass for sunsets on most clear evenings, this is Tal-y-llyn, or Llyn Myngul. On its far shore is the Ty'n y Gornel hotel once the mecca for anglers in this area. In his 1925 book 'In praise of North Wales' the once famous doyen of this angling world, and author of several other books, A.G. Bradley reminisces about his role in this golden age of gentlemen anglers when he was a young man. His account of the cosy comradeship these privileged gentlemen of leisure enjoyed in the late Victorian period at the Ty'n y Gornel includes an account of a curious if not extraordinary incident which occurred one June day in 1882.

A passing traveller happened to glance at Llyn y Tri Greyenyn one early morning and was more than surprised to see a huge dorsal fin breaking the surface of the water! He called at the Ty'n y Gornel to impart his news but was apparently met with ridicule and his account certainly not taken seriously. One Dr. Frere Webb however decided to walk up to the little lake and 'have a look'. He used a live minnow as bait and on his very first cast he hooked and landed a 5lb brown trout!

When one considers that no stream either entered or left the lake which was sited at 850 feet above sea level and was little more than a large rain puddle the presence of any fish let alone a magnificent specimen of 5lbs beggars belief!

The smoke room at the Ty'n y Gornel must have been alight with questions and speculations that evening.

How had it got there?

Had anyone put it in?

Was the passing traveller responsible?

Was Dr. Webb having an elaborate joke?

Unfortunately there is no record that anyone examined its stomach contents, an act which would have been a logical step towards solving the mystery. Webb however did make a life size

The three 'pebbles'

Carving on garden wall

water colour painting of the fish and when Bradley had last visited the hotel around 1902 it had still been there adorning the lounge wall.

So, not only did I have a vanished lake to look for but a painting as well!

The trip down to Mid Wales in fair weather is always a joy and in less than two hours I was parking in the lay-by opposite where the lake used to be. Having studied the site of the lake, looked for its different coloured rushes and the three 'pebbles' removed from a giant's sandal I decided to get a photograph from above. The steep climb up the scree towards the summit of Craig y Llam gave me a good overview of the stage where this drama occurred, and by the time I got back to the car I certainly felt a coffee at the Ty'n y Gornel would be more than justified.

Whilst driving down the valley beneath the continuation of the cliff the huge singular block of stone appears, perched precariously above the road. Which in keeping with the crag's sinister theme has been named the Devil's Pulpit.

It was very much an 'angling' hotel and had recently been acquired as the flagship by Welsh Water to further promote fishing in Wales. There were boats on Tal-y-llyn lake, their occupants gently whipping the water with their flies as they drifted across. A couple of empty ones lay nodding at their moorings yards from the hotel entrance. Carvings of giant trout caught in years past adorned the low slate walls outside and bamboo fishing rods, wooden reels and creel baskets decorated various corners inside. The walls contained themed pictures of lakes, bearded anglers and large fish. I ordered a coffee and started looking for the one painted by Dr. Frere Webb in 1882.

My initial search failed to find it so I had my coffee and decided to ask the manager if he had any inkling about its whereabouts.

"No" he couldn't recall seeing it. So I told him the story.

"There are some old pictures in the back" he said, "Do you want to come and have a look?" He showed me into a storage room which contained a couple of dusty tables, some broken chairs, cleaning materials and half a dozen framed pictures leaning against the wall in one corner. I looked through them and almost immediately found the giant trout from the 'Three Pepple Pool'. It was an 'eureka' moment in which he too became enthusiastic, declaring he would put it back in its rightful place on the wall. I even had another coffee on the house as I re-told the story to the staff. We both agreed that it would be highly unlikely that the mystery of how the fish got into the lake would ever be solved but the story deserved preserving, it was as much a part of local fishing folklore as anything on display.

This happened over thirty years ago and over a hundred years after the event itself.

I recently called at the Ty'n y Gornel and was struck by a marked change. No longer are the fishing rods and creels stamping its mark as a fishing hotel and the lake appeared empty of boats. The clientele now comprised of lunching families and reserved elderly couples sipping their cappuccinos, things seemed very different. Upon enquiring it seems the policy of only allowing barbless hooks and having to return all catches had destroyed the hotel's attraction for anglers. Bradley, must have spun in his grave.

But... still hanging, and appropriately on the wall nearest the lake is the giant trout from 'Three Pebble Pool' telling its own story and playing its own part in maintaining the memory of a once vibrant angling community and their rich tradition.

The fish

Chapter 3

The Welsh Houdini

This is quite a sad story about a man who didn't get the best starts in life and spent it stumbling from one authority defying episode to another. In modern parlance he would be called a 'loser' and although most of his problems were of his own doing one cannot help feel some sympathy for this 'character' who came from a little village near Bala.

Coch Bach y Bala

The diminutive figure pathetically shuffling up the steep field from Nantclwyd Isaf farm, Pwll-glas, clad only in prison underpants, an old sack and a dirty overcoat was a sorry sight. A young man of nineteen carrying a shotgun was also close by and was having no trouble keeping up with him. According to his later testament he was trying to persuade the older man to give himself up. John Jones, better known as 'Coch Bach y Bala' had escaped from Ruthin gaol five days earlier whilst awaiting transfer to Stafford prison to serve a 3 year sentence. He was sixty years old and had spent forty two of them in prison.

Born in Llanfor, Bala in 1854 he had been brought up by his grandmother in what was for them, a very austere world. Stealing eggs had been his introduction to crime and there is a record of him being flogged by the police at the age of six for stealing a candle! By the time he was fourteen he was an accomplished poacher and already a notorious petty thief. Despite this growing notoriety the slight, red haired youth was a popular figure around Bala.

It was in 1871 that he received his first taste of incarceration when he was gaoled for a month for poaching.

In 1872 he received his first prison sentence of note and was gaoled for four months for stealing an empty purse, a pocket knife and weighing scales, all worthless trinkets; a curious pattern which was to repeat itself many times over the years.

He enjoyed the ignomy and reputation and would hide his loot in walls and hedges. Many suspected that some of the items he revealed to chosen friends as evidence of his prowess as a thief may not have actually been stolen!

In 1873 he stole a padlock, a shilling (5p), and an old penny from a house in Llandrillo as well as half a sovereign, three groat pieces, three threepenny bits, a farling and another padlock from a house in Corwen. Two relatively worthless hauls which possibly pointed to a medical problem rather than any real planning for ill gotten riches. For his troubles Dolgellau Quarter Sessions court gave him six years! Some of this sentence was served in English prisons. Six years from the prime of his life for stealing the equivelant of 75p! No wonder his bitterness towards the authorities were vented in full on the prison officers as he was led away.

Following good behavious he was out on licence in 1878 but within a few weeks, following his involvement in a toll gate altercation he was one of five given 6 months prison; Coch Bach was to spend his sixth Christmas behind bars.

By now he was a larger than life figure in the Dee valley and parents would threaten their children with him if they didn't behave; he was the bogey man of the 1870s!

In 1879 when he was arrested again it is recorded that he was working in some capacity with timber. He was given three months gaol when he was picked up near Gresford Wood Yard for 'being a rogue and a vagabond'! By now he was understandably extremely bitter with the Authorities as once again he was incarcerated in Chester and Rhuthun gaols. I wonder what sort of evidence was needed in 1879 to convict him of being a 'rogue and a vagabond' or was it a case of being Coch Bach y Bala in the wrong place at the wrong time?

He was released on the 10th October but was arrested again within four days! This time thirteen watches had been stolen from the home of one John Richards, Llanycil who owned a watch shop in Bala. Coch had been seen in the possession of two watches and a witness testified to his buying drink in the old Woolpack Inn, Oswestry. As always John denied the charge claiming he was in the Ffestiniog area at the time and proceeded

Rhuthun goal

to present to the Magistrate's court an extremely rambling statement to that effect. Despite a typically lengthy and largely irrelevant discourse no proof was offered that a friend had given him the watches. It was therefore inevitable that he was remanded in Rhuthun gaol to await the next Quarter Sessions which would not be until January!

On the night of November 30th he perpetrated an amazing escape from the gaol, the first of five which he was to execute over the ensuing years. Somehow he managed to not only open his own cell door but three others and whilst the warders were having their supper he walked out through the front gates of the prison as bold as brass. This daring escapade was to make the national papers and a five pounds reward was offered for his capture.

At this point common sense should have convinced him to seek his future far away from his native Wales, but not John; he returned to Llanfor of all places!

Inevitably, a break-in which occurred on December 7th was blamed on him, it had all his hallmarks (or MO in modern parlance). Penucha'r Llan farmhouse, Llanfor had been burgled whilst the occupants were in chapel and a purse, two padlocks, a knife and almost forty pounds had been stolen.

By now legends were beginning to grow around him. One describes the local policeman going to his old home in Llanfor to look for him only to turn away when he looked through the window and saw an old lady in a shawl sitting in front of the fire; of course this was later claimed to have been John! Another rumour claimed he had a hideaway beneath the hearth stone. Darker tales were spun describing John breaking into a house to steal the pennies from the eyes of a corpse awaiting burial! There were claims he had burgled houses in Bala, Llanuwchllyn and on the slopes of the Aran; all at the same time. There is no doubt that Coch Bach y Bala was blamed for some crimes he didn't commit. Records show that in one three month period in 1879 sixty people had been sent to Rhuthun Gaol; a sure indication that crime was not a rarity!

The Quarter Sessions which should have dealt with John were due in January and the Authorities were obviously most anxious to find and re-capture him. The rumour mill continued to grind with one story anticipating John would be present at court in disguise to see his own trial!

On January 3rd however, no doubt following a tip off John was arrested in the Swan Inn, Mochdre whilst he was still in bed. The arresting officer was his old enemy William Jones.

Following another lengthy trial in which he represented himself and accused the police and William Jones in particular of hounding him and blaming him for every misdemeanor which occurred he was given the substantial sentence of fourteen years. Such was the considered magnitude of John's capture and his embarrassing weeks of freedom that William Jones was awarded three pounds by the court! John went down vowing revenge on his old foe and promising to escape again. He had lived like a lord at The Swan Inn wearing a tail coat and kid gloves; the next few years which he would spend in Pentonville and Dartmoor would not be as comfortable.

One amusing little anecdote which occurred during his period of freedom concerns a wealthy businessman in Llanycil who had hidden his gold so safely he had the temerity to openly dare John to steal it. Of course the gold was alleged to have been stolen and one of the upshots of this was for John's photograph to appear on posters all over the country advertising for people to keep their money safe in the bank!

Despite an attempt to escape early on he settled to the grim Dartmoor regime and eventually Coch Bach y Bala was released in 1891. He did not on this occasion return to his native Bala. Instead he spent a few months as a stoker aboard ship and travelled to Buenos Aires, and Antwerp, a period in his life whose details have always been a little vague. He then turned up in Middlesborough and was caught pawning a watch in Essex which he had stolen. When apprehended on the street he feigned an arthritic limp on the way to the police station only

Swan Inn, Mochdre

to suddenly sprint away leaving the arresting policemen standing! It was only because an ex-boxer, one Henry Duffin (you couldn't make this surname up!) happened to be nearby that he was caught!

He was also suspected of other burglaries involving the theft of a knife and a padlock, objects known to attract the little Welshman. He was brought up before Judge Hawkins at the high court and for the first time in his 'judicial career' he pleaded guilty and was duly given five years. And then, bizarrely following some rough handling on his way down to the cells when he retaliated and exchanged blows with the custody officers he was recalled and given another two years; all seven to be served in Dartmoor! Whilst there is little doubt John Jones could be his own worst enemy it is also quite apparent that he received a lot of harsh treatment at the hands of the authorities. His story certainly supports the old saying 'Give a dog a bad name'.

Once again in this litany of alternating between gaol and freedom John's good behaviour was to see him released after five years and this is when his longest period of freedom took place, four years of not offending, (or not getting caught)! Although the exact details of how he spent these four years are uncertain it is most likely that he went to sea again.

In 1900 he turned up in Amlwch and took lodgings with a Mrs. Hughes in Well Street where the fickle finger of fate was waiting once again for John. He was in the Waterman's Arms one evening when he asked Jane Owen the landlady to change a sovereign. John noticed that Jane went upstairs to do this and correctly assumed that it was where the money was kept. When ten pounds were discovered missing Coch Bach y Bala was instantly and naturally suspected. He was taken to Beaumaris gaol to await his Magistrate court appearance and then to Caernarfon gaol to await the Assizes in three months time.

As usual John conducted his own defence. The main piece of evidence offered by the police was a bootprint found on the floor upstairs. His eloquence and cross examination techniques had improved considerably since his last Welsh court appearance in 1880. Unfortunately, rather than focussing on discrediting this evidence as flimsy he launched into a long winded tirade against the police and accused them of placing his boot prints there. This was tantamount to admitting they actually were his boot prints, John had shot himself in the foot once again! He was found guilty and given five years on top of which he would have to serve an extra two and a half years to cover the parole period he had been released early for good behavior!

Whilst in Caernarfon goal awaiting his move to Dartmoor a night of celebration took place nationwide for the relief of Mafeking in the Boer war. The Welsh Houdini decided that he too would celebrate by escaping once again. Unfortunately having dug through the floor of his cell one of the guards heard him and he was caught before he could make his getaway! He was to spend the next six years in Dartmoor.

Four years after the trial a sock containing ten pounds was discovered hidden in a hedge near Amlwch and Jane Owen was able to produce the sock's partner; final evidence if it was needed of Coch Bach's guilt!

We next hear of him in 1906 working on the new harbour in Pwllheli. by now he was 42 years old and he had spent 35 of them behind bars! There is evidence to suggest he was a popular figure with his workmates during what was possibly the happiest period of his woeful life. He lodged with a Hannah Jones in South Beach and seemed content to live a normal life. Unfortunately a storm which would threaten his very life was about to break upon him.

In the nearby village of Aber-erch seventy one year old Sarah Jones had gone upstairs to investigate a noise she had heard one afternoon and was surprised to see a man hiding under the bed. She attempted to run away but was overtaken on the stairs and in the struggle was knocked unconscious. Ten pounds had been stolen and Coch Bach was immediately suspected, especially as he had been laid off work a couple of days previously.

He was remanded in Caernarfon gaol to await Sarah's recovery before appearing before Pwllheli Magistrates, it would be five weeks before a case against him was ready. Despite an ID parade she failed to pick him out and despite several confusing and contradictory testimonies he was charged with assault. As usual although the gravity of the case against him was serious he decided to represent himself and because of this it would go down as one of the most unusual trials in British history. At one point John halted proceedings to ask for a cup of tea...which was granted! And then, due to his insistence on drawing out a long summing up speech referring to several irrelevant and inappropriate points he had laboured over during the trial the case went on until 4.00am! The final decision was that he should go before the Assizes and was duly remanded in Caernarfon gaol once again for another four months!

When the case was eventually heard John was found guilty

and was to spend the next seven years once again in Dartmoor before being released for the last time on January 24th 1913.

Tales are told that every station between Ruabon and Pwllheli were manned by a policeman supervising his return journey from Dartmoor when he returned to register his parole at Pwllheli police station.

When he returned to Bala many who still remembered him feted him and even welcomed him in a subdued way and he was given work by John Owen of the White Lion painting and looking after pleasure boats on the lake. As the weeks turned to months many hoped he had finally settled to live out the rest of his life as simply as possible, but Friday June 6th was to dissolve that hope for ever!

Coch Bach was accused of breaking into an office in Bala belonging to a Mr. Jordan who was a solicitor. A hastily convened Magistrate's court decreed he could be kept in the police cells until Monday. Sometime on Saturday night he managed to break a water pipe and remove stones around it to leave a hole no larger than a foot square through which he escaped; once again he had lived up to one of his aliases, the Welsh Houdini! Many people joined in the search with several claiming to have 'only just missed him' in a few locations. He was finally caught on Tuesday evening in the cowshed of Tyncelyn farm, Pant-glas, no more than three miles from Bala, he hadn't eaten since Saturday.

One can sense the overriding hopelessness and inevitability which consumed this pathetic middle aged man as he stumbled from one mishap to the other driven by feral instincts and there is little wonder that many carried a lot of sympathy for Coch Bach.

True to form he conducted his own defence when his case eventually came up before the Quarter Sessions. By this time the only charge he faced was breaking and entering which was based on a red handkerchief found on the scene. He cross examined the witnesses with a mixture of sensible and ludicrous questions and managed to make his summing up last from half ten until five o'clock. To no avail; once again he was sentenced to three years and sent to Rhuthun gaol. John appealed but was turned down leaving him a very resentful and embittered figure once again.

Months passed and it seemed to the prison authorities that John had accepted his lot, when he was told one day he was to be moved to Stafford gaol. That night he managed to make a small hole in his cell wall and using sheets to make a rope he lowered himself on to the chapel roof before he worked his way along the outer wall and jumped down into a hay rick on the outside. He had done it again!

Without food he had no strength to go very far and a couple of sightings confirmed him to still be in the area. A loaf and some methylated spirits were stolen from Bryn Obwst farm. He even approached a couple of farms to beg, one turned him away and he lost his nerve in the other when the farmer went inside to actually fetch some food and ran away.

And so Coch Bach y Bala clothed as a scarecrow, tired, hungry and desperate after 5 days on the run is approaching Coppice Woods above Nantclwyd Isaf farm closely shadowed by 19 year old Reginald John Bateman of Euarth House. When Coch Bach reached the woods Bateman alleges he tried once more to persuade him to give up but claims John reached into his pocket for what Bateman feared was a gun. At that point Bateman shot him in the leg and within a few minutes John Jones, Coch Bach y Bala, the Welsh Houdini had bled to death. It was the sorry end to a sorry life.

Reginald Bateman

Having cycled up from Pwll-glas one spring morning along the

Where he was killed

beautiful country lanes weaving through this modest upland I made my way along a footpath through the woodland growing on the limestone bluff above the upper Clwyd valley, I could see Nantclwyd Isaf farm far below. I had with me an old black and white photograph and I managed to locate the exact spot where John was shot and killed. The trees in early bloom and the pungent smell of wild garlic makes it an attractive location. That attraction however was somewhat tainted by the knowledge of what had happened there just over a century earlier. It is a sad melancholic spot and the only positive thought I could inject into my reflections was that John had died out in the free open countryside rather than behind the grim walls of a prison where the odds dictated to be the most likely place he would draw his final breath.

Due to a technical point, because he had been free for more than two days the responsibility for his burial fell on the parish rather than the prison service and John Jones was laid to rest in Llanelidan cemetery where he would eventually find the rest he could never manage to find during his life.

Bateman came from a family of wealthy landowners and despite being charged with manslaughter, inexplicably he never stood trial. Notwithstanding that they were an unpopular family there were also some very strong feelings about what he had done. It was widely believed that he had discharged both barrels at John and many thought he should have stood trial for murder. When the Great War broke out the following year three of the Bateman brothers, Reginald, Francis and Llywelyn joined up and were commissioned to Welsh regiments.

Francis and Llywelyn were both killed in action with a strong rumour that his own men had shot Francis due to his unpopularity. Rumour also claimed that a grenade accident which injured Reginald was also caused by his own men. Whether these stories are true or not is important only because they exist; demonstrating perhaps that what happened to Coch Bach had not been forgiven. Even if the rumours were more a statement of desire than what actually happened it shows that feelings still ran high over the final pathetic fate of John Jones of Llanfor.

Following a couple of newspaper and television articles chronicling his story, interest in Coch Bach y Bala was briefly revived in the 1960s which resulted in a collection of twenty one pounds which was raised to provide the simplest of gravestones for the likeable old rogue fifty years after he was laid to rest.

John Jones' grave

Chapter 4

The Forbidden Beach

In the last chapter I described a journey, first by car, then by bike and finally through the colourful woods of a Clwyd Valley to visit a melancolic spot where one of Wales' 'characters' ended his life. This chapter describes a voyage entirely by kayak to a special somewhere I wouldn't have been allowed to visit any other way.

Ynys Llanddwyn

My kayak on the beach

I would like to share with you a quiet, yellow and turquoise world which I was able to access only with my kayak a few summers ago.

Anglesey has an excellent coastal path which circumnavigates the whole island, diligently hugging the entire shoreline with two notable exceptions. One, naturally enough includes a mile or so where Wylfa Nuclear Power Station (now de-commissioned) dominates the shore line where it once drew water for its reactors. The other is the Bodorgan estate, an area the size of Rhyl which has a balanced mixture of grazing meadows and streams, sand dunes and marsh, and a magnificent rocky coastline which even has an ancient fort, but is totally devoid of public access. It has some of the cleanest, loveliest and of course the loneliest beaches on the island. It was here within its guarded confines that the royal couple were housed when Prince William did his helicopter rescue training at RAF Valley, influenced no doubt by his Aunt Sarah's 'Budgie the Helicopter' books. How would one even begin to measure the investment value of this indulgence for the British tax payer?

The Bodorgan estate owned by the same family since the

Norman conquest when it was gifted for services rendered, is one of the few large Anglesey estates to survive the modern world. It has been linked with the Meyrick family for many generations.

There are six of these beaches on this very private stretch of coast, five are named on the OS map. Porth can mean a port, entrance, but in this context is used to mean a cove or a bay. They are:- Porth y Gro (Bay of Gravel), Porth Twyn-Mawr (Large Dune Bay), Porth y Cwch (Boat Bay), Porth Cae Ceffylau (Bay of the Field of Horses), and Porth Cadwaladr (Cadwaladr's Bay). On the map they look extremely alluring and forbidden access from landward did not sit comfortably with me.

Anyway, that was the setting, and I was determined to visit these 'forbidden' beaches for myself!

My understanding was that land below the high water mark belongs to the crown and unless there are specific decrees issued because of nuclear instalments, (see above), military

A view from the sand dunes

usage, or the anthrax infested island of Gruinard off the coast of Scotland (up to 1990 anyway) the public have a right to be there. So, clinging to this doctrine as a talisman which would have hopefully prevented my incarceration in the 'Tower' as tightly as I clung to my paddle I set off from a crowded Newborough beach in my trusty kayak.

Someone once said of a journey that it's not the arrival but the getting there which holds the joy; on this near perfect day eight years ago I can honestly say it was both.

The first few strokes to clear the foot high surf were untidy as I pushed through the shallow frothy soup; and then it felt

My kayak with sail

good as the paddles bit in deeper water and I surged forward. Soon the cries of shrieking children were left behind as I warmed to my task aiming for a distant buoy beckoning some four hundred yards ahead. Passing it told me the strength and direction of the flow as I picked my next target which could have been another buoy, a plastic bottle or a patch of seaweed as long as it was in line with the distant tip of Ynys Llanddwyn.

Before long I spotted several jellyfish of varying sizes, a sad indictment of the global pollution we were responsible for. As the least tactile and approachable of our sea denizens it is also unfortunately, the most adaptable and is positively thriving in this pollution. A cormorant somewhere to my left decided I was getting too close and dived to emerge in a few seconds behind me whilst on the rocks on the distant Llanddwyn headland its cousins stood drying their wings like a 'downside up' row of bats.

I had settled into a comfortable rhythm by the time I reached this popular high tide island with its two distinct but redundant lighthouses standing like white sentinels at each end of its outer shore. I passed a couple of rocky islets surrounded in white surf to my left and drew level with the two mini beaches on the main island. Here can be found cowrie shells with some patient searching in the sand around the foot of the ancient Cambrian bedrock itself interspersed with streaks and bubbles of red jasper. It is a magical place and even in winter storms, invariably, there will be someone there. From here I could espy the next headland two miles away, where, beyond lay the goal of my day's voyage.

At this point I should issue a note of caution, paddling this open two mile crossing of Malltraeth bay is a commitment best tackled in company.

I exchanged a friendly wave with someone walking the rocks above as I paused for a drink. The twenty five minute paddle here was just a warm up, the next section would be more serious but was to be relished. I set off aiming for the distant hazy head

Jasper

of Pen Dinas three quarters of an hour away passing a couple of lobster buoys as I left the last of Llanddwyn's satellite islets and resigned myself to look for floating seaweed, fishing cormorants, or the odd piece of driftwood as my targets and companions for the next forty five minutes. My mind soon kicked into neutral, chasing whichever thoughts presented themselves as my shoulders pulled and pushed, left, right, left, right over a moving world of green, blue and white as I slowly made my way across the bay.

The swell was slight and the breeze almost in my face, I hoped it would remain, so that I could use my folding sail to come back. The occasional hissing white topped wave which splashed my face had the inevitable salty taste and left a white crusty residue as it dried on my cheeks. The restless moving stage on which I was enacting my own personal drama reflected the azure cloudless sky. The Malltraeth sand dunes a mile to my right looked warm and inviting and the rocky cliffs of Pen-y-Parc were definitely coming closer; life was good!

Just then a diving tern ahead caught my eye, and then another, there must be whiting. And where there's whiting there may be mackerel! Could my luck be in? I quickly paddled over and unwound the weighted line which I always keep in the kayak, letting the four hooks festooned with shiny foil and feathers sink about three fathoms.

Ten minutes investment as puppet master of this dancing glitter might provide me with a mackerel lunch. And did it too? Within seconds I could feel the unmistakable quivering of a hooked fish and soon had the writhing, glinting forms safely in my cockpit larder! Anyone who has ever fished for mackerel and stumbled upon a kamikaze shoal will know how impossible it is not to catch them; but they will also know the first few minutes of pulse racing excitement when this happens. It only took three dances and I kept only the four largest, as, enough is as good as a feast and in less than my self-allocated ten minutes was under way again to the accompaniment of screaming seagulls who had become, for a while at least my new best friends.

A small rocky island seen only at low water appeared on my right, Caseg Malltraeth (The Malltraeth Mare) no doubt a reference to the white horses formed when the waves broke over the rocks. Its arrival was a sure sign that I had almost completed the crossing. Landlubbers would have said I was now approaching the headland, sailors would say I was raising it, much as I had been sinking Llanddwyn Island for the best part of an hour. Lobster buoys once again presented themselves as I found myself paddling beneath the ruined ramparts of Trwyn y Parc Iron Age fort which, perversely still seemed to be guarding this beautiful corner of Ynys Mon against the public. It was interesting to reflect that the Romans had also made use of these old battlements for their own mysterious purpose.

The crags of Pen-y-Parc now reared above me in stark contrast to my recent open crossing. Buttresses and gullies rose from a swaying base of yellow-brown seaweed to reach for the old fort somewhere on top. An old football jammed into a crack

One of the beaches

and the mangled remains of a lobster pot which had been hurled on to a tiny ledge a storm or two ago caught my eye. Its green polypropylene rope lay draped like a giant strand of a spider's web and led across the wave roughened rocks to a miniature fjord cutting deep into the cliffs. I paddled on. A few more strokes and there it was, two hundred metres away, the first of the forbidden beaches. I turned the kayak's nose and paddled in.

The transparent water in this lonely cove was as clear as it gets, the sand on the shelving bottom looked clean and pristine as I stopped paddling and let my kayak glide the last few feet and gently grate itself to a halt on to the khaki sand. I sat there a few seconds gently rocked by wavelets, soaking the sun on my back and simply relishing my arrival, and the serenity which pervaded this 'world' which I would borrow for an hour or so. The tiny bay was cosily embraced on both sides by rocks rising perhaps thirty feet, the back of the beach morphed into sand dunes which in turn gave way to pasture with the odd outcrop of rock. One corner contained an array of flotsam ranging from colourful plastic containers, ropes and nets to an useful choice of driftwood. Three thin collars of seaweed running parallel along the sand told its own tale of receding tides and the sea glimmered where it met the sun as thousands of dancing sparks melted and existed for mere nanoseconds.

A nearby rock in the other corner would be my 'bistro'. Clearing a patch of dried seaweed, black and crackly with little jumping flies I soon had a fire going and using what appeared to be an old rudder as a table had the mackerel gutted and prepared. The resulting feast was an accidental mixture of fresh and smoked – perfect! Apart from a few of my erstwhile best friends who had returned it was impressively tranquil, with only the rhythmic lapping of sea and sand meeting and greeting hypnotically emphasizing the silence. A passing yacht hugging the far off horizon was barely moving, accentuating my remoteness, I felt so privileged. I idly imagined a future king and his princess paddling in these turquoise shallows, barefeet and holding hands in their own private down time a world away from shaking hands, curtsies and clicking cameras. I stayed there an hour exploring the rocks and sand dunes, beachcombing and taking photographs knowing even as I took them that they could never capture the special magic I had enjoyed so far that day. And then, I knew it was time to break the spell, clear up and go, but knowing too that one day I would come back.

These beaches are enchanting, each within its own cove, each as beautiful as its neighbour and each one empty. I didn't visit them all, just 'looked in' as I paddled past. And then quietly mouthing an 'adieu' I trimmed my sail and pointed my little craft east at the distant headland of Ynys Llanddwyn, my paddle now used only as a rudder; because the breeze had stayed! An incident free almost anti climatic return journey where I barely used a dozen strokes in 'raising' Llanddwyn completed a perfect day.

I had reached 'my forbidden beaches', enjoyed the beautiful solitude they offered, and feasted like a king on crown land! And to cap the irony the second in line to the throne lived just a sand dune or three away, I wonder if he could smell the mackerel?

Chapter 5

Mari the Witch

I was particularly intrigued to read about this character, especially as it was strongly implied that photographs taken of her ruined cottage, failed to develop!

MARI THE WITCH

The Kite I saw in the air

One dictionary definition of a witch is 'a woman who has dealings with evil spirits and practises the black art of sorcery'. Another alludes to women who are 'fascinating and bewitchin' whilst yet another subscribes to the fairy tale image of 'old and ugly hags'. Most fairy tales have evil witches who fly on besoms with black cats, have an intimate knowledge of potions made of plants, with toads and snakes somehow being part of the recipe. Literature rarely concedes the existence of good witches.

Society, intolerant as it is, has always found ways to persecute anyone who is different, and in 1736 an act was passed which legitimized the persecution of witches. Many innocent women were blamed for dying cattle and sickening children, and died cruel deaths at the hands, in many cases of their own neighbours. Thankfully, ducking stools, and other pro-active punishments for women whom society couldn't understand gradually waned towards the end of the nineteenth century; and eventually the act was repealed in 1951. This wasn't to say of course, that witches ceased to exist!

I have in my possession a collection of magazines going back sixty years containing articles on a variety of topics related to Wales and the Borders. One, written many decades ago tells of Mari, a real life witch who was buried in Llanbadarn Trefeglwys churchyard near the village of Pennant, Cardiganshire in 1896.

There are of course several books with tales of Welsh witches, but the one element in this particular story which caught my imagination was that despite attempts to photograph Berllan Biter, her now ruined cottage; the photos just did not come out! There were also incidents cited when dogs refused to enter or children became distressed for no apparent reason; and all these when Mari had been dead for over eighty years.

So, predictably I planned a day down there to look for this ruined cottage which lay somewhere in a wooded valley south of Aberystwyth; and of course to take a photo!

But first thing's first; I had to get at least a rough idea of the location as modern OS maps tend not to mark small ruined

Llanbadarn church

cottages. Perhaps, after 38 years, the ruin might not even be there. Having trawled through my personal library, I had whittled the probable site down to being somewhere on the banks of the river Arth; venturing on to Google reinforced my conviction. I had almost accepted the search would be a combination of a speculative knock on a farm door, or following a river valley with all the bogs, brambles and barbed wire it might entail, and then I had a break! Whilst searching through some old tithe maps, I found it; Berllan, complete with its own paddock, and reassuringly almost exactly where I suspected it would be, if I'd had a tail it would have wagged. A few days later I set off.

It was a crisp and clear January day and the trip down through Rhuthun, Bala and Machynlleth was a treat. I stopped for a coffee in the little community café in Tre'r-Ddol, and half an hour after negotiating Aberystwyth's one way system I was parking the car beside Llanbadarn church; it was twelve o'clock.

I had already decided to think myself into a witch-seeking mode, and be suitably tuned in to any 'vibes' which might have been still humming around the old cottage. Adopting this temporary role of a benign witch-hunter general had the side effect of making me acutely aware of other factors which may influence my mission; for example would my presence be welcome in this lonely wooded valley? So, being the proverbial stranger in a strange land and therefore not privy to any contentious trespass issues, or touchy landowners, I'd chosen a route which, although longer, kept me on public rights of way, certainly until I got under the cover of the trees.

The walking was pleasant, initially along a country lane with grass in the middle and tree roots exposed at the sides, I didn't encounter any cars. I spotted and photographed a kite dancing on the thermals in the sky above which was looking for its lunch, or was it a reincarnated Mari still watching over her cottage? Soon I reached a farm track I needed to follow and left the tarmac to weave in between several puddles for some three hundred metres. Eventually I picked up the footpath whose signage lacked enthusiasm at best, and headed across a wet open field past a bungalow, feeling very exposed. The field was pockmarked with cattle hoofs, a thousand squelching saucers of water just waiting for me to stumble as I picked a route towards the trees four hundred yards away.

Unhindered by any challenging shouts, rampaging bullocks, or shotgun pellets I reached a stile and was soon safely swallowed in an attractive deciduous woodland which almost immediately began dropping to the valley floor and the river Arth 400 metres away and some 300 feet lower.

As I descended the old overgrown track, it occurred to me that Mari and her contemporaries would have walked that way many times, some no doubt approaching her cottage with dread. Soon, I reached a bend in the old track, and with a tingle of anticipation began looking down to my right hoping there would be something left to see. I needn't have fretted; the gable end of Mari's cottage appeared quite suddenly, smothered in a chaotic jumble of fallen trees. Berllan Biter was perched on a natural

Lane approaching Berllan

Ash growing out of chimney

Gable end of the cottage

shelf, barely wider than the cottage itself, overlooking the slope which continued for another hundred metres down to the river.

It was but a shell; a huge sycamore grew in one corner, and a couple of ash trees had sprouted from both chimneys. Two signs outside warned against trespass, but I hadn't driven for two and a half hours to heed those. In front, and on the valley floor an ancient paddock was now a thicket of hazel and willow groves. It must only have been two rooms with possibly a crog loft. I'll swerve a detailed description of the old ruin and let the photographs show what is left. Yes, it seemed the old dear's powers had either worn off after 121 years or her spells didn't stretch to digital cameras. I sat down and opened my thermos, to reflect on all I'd read about Mari the witch.

She was born in 1817, here in Berllan Biter where she lived

with her parents John and Mary Davies, John is recorded as having worked as a gardener for nearby Mynachdy. When her parents died, she stayed on, and lived here all her life, only moving to the village of Aber-Arth to be nursed for the last year of her old age.

Another version claims she was born in 1824, and originally came from Llangurig; an area renowned for its withcraft; it is hinted she may even have had a daughter there.

Of slight build she never grew much taller than four foot; she carried a stick, and was always seen wearing a shawl over her shoulders along with an old hat, which, because most people were taller, always seemed to hide her face. She fitted the stereotype of a witch, a strange woman living alone, deep in the woods, and no doubt deliberately contributed to this reputation herself. It was even claimed she could change into a hare! Mari could be cantankerous and strong willed at times, and several tales are told to illustrate why falling out with her was to be avoided.

One story tells how her cousin John Pwll-glas, left some corn for her at the edge of the woods late one evening, rather than make his tired old mare Bess negotiate the steep path down to her cottage. The next morning Bess couldn't get up in the stable. Suspecting Mari was somehow responsible, she was sent for; but denied being the cause of Bess's immobility. She did, however whisper a few words in Bess's ear, and the old mare suddenly got up on her feet. On another occasion, she suspected three men who were working in the field nearby of killing one of her hens by forcing a snail down its throat. They denied having done it, and laughed when confronted by Mari. Over the next few days, each one of them lost one of his cattle.

Thomas Gruffydd the miller in Pennant was about to start grinding the last load of the day, when Mari turned up demanding that her barley needed doing there and then. He explained he would do it first thing in the morning, but she wasn't satisfied and stormed off. No sooner had she gone that the flour refused to come down the hopper, and the wheels of the mill started turning the wrong way! He had to chase after her and promise to do her grinding straight away. When they both returned to the mill ten minutes later everything was back to normal.

Another time, when she was refused a little butter in Ynys-Hir farm, she retorted that any attempt to churn butter that afternoon would fail, and she was right.

Mari had her good points too; she was apparently very good with animals; and on more than one occasion could persuade a horse which had hitherto lay down and refused to drag its load to get up and continue. It was always Mari that Lluest Pennant farm called when milk refused to churn, she would give the barrel a slight tap, mutter a few words and all would be well

Tales are told of how she kept snakes in dry leaves in her cottage, and she once apparently divulged how she made her spells, using a ball of wool with pins which floated in a basin of water. She kept special verses in her Bible for such purposes. Although a regular attender at Pennant chapel, her presence was always met with a degree of reservation. She had her own pew which no-one would share, and children would avoid it at all cost. It must have been a strange, lonely life to live on the periphery of such a rural Victorian society, relying, I would suggest on the enigma of her reputation to survive as a woman living alone, in so remote a spot.

Mari died in late July 1896 and was buried in Llanbadarn churchyard in a white deal coffin on the 12th of August. She was carried in a trap for her final journey drawn ironically, by Bess her cousin's old mare.

I drained the last of my coffee, took a moment to listen as the birds of Berllan woods chirped in the winter sunshine. They seemed to sing to the accompaniment of the musical flow of the river tinkling over the smooth stones, as if they were piano keys, reinforcing my opinion of what a wonderful place to have had a cottage and to live a lifetime in it. I wondered too whether Mari

Pennant chapel

would have enjoyed the same sights, the same smells, and appreciated the same tranquility that I was blessed with right then. Despite being 'open' to any lingering echoe of Mari's presence, the serenity of the spot was the closest I got to Mari Berllan Biter. I was almost disappointed to have captured a digital image of her old cottage, an indication perhaps, that her bewitching influence had finally gone.

My way back was across the river, over a delightful little footbridge and up the opposite bank past an ancient iron age fort. I briefly examined its undulating ruins, and wondered about the stories it could tell if only earthen parapets could talk. My way continued relying on a little navigation along footpaths not used very often, before I emerged at the little village of Pennant. I passed Mari's chapel and Thomas Gruffydd's mill (now a private house) and forty minutes after leaving Mari's cottage, I was back at the car.

I did have a quick look around the cemetery, but knew I would find no grave for Mari. She was buried at the time when headstones were for those who could afford them, and Mari Davies of Berllan Biter would not have been one of those privileged few.

And then, just before I got in the car I spotted what might have been a kite in the distance hovering in the air above Berllan woods!

All I had to do now was get home without losing the camera or dropping it in water!

Chapter 6

Ogwen

It is easy to take somewhere one uses as a starting point, or passes through, for granted without realizing just how many things of interest can be seen so close to the car. In this chapter I have tried to describe some such things in a location used by so many merely as a springboard for the higher mountains.

View of Tryfan

The word 'Ogwen' has almost become a bye-word in the mountaineering world for soaring three thousand foot peaks rising from the scenic lake lying beside the highest point of the A5. Generations of rockclimbers have learnt how to thrutch up polished slabs worn smooth by decades of nailed boots. Thousands of people park here every year and set off for their days out in the mountains; and why not?

How many of these thousands of climbers and walkers though have considered investing half a day and spending some time exploring Ogwen itself?

In over sixty years my visits to Ogwen, or to use its original name 'Y Benglog' can be numbered in the hundreds and in the following pages I would like to share some interesting and historical places I consider worth seeking out in the immediate area where you park your vehicle.

Rather than go back to the last Ice Age when 'Y Benglog' was formed I shall begin my narrative just over two centuries ago in the form of a half day's walk.

You must arrive early on a summer's weekend to find a space in the car park under the trees at the lower end of the lake.

The snack bar and toilet block which also houses the

Old tea shack from the 70s

Hone stone quarry

Warden's office and a modest Information room was built in 2014 to replace its predecessor which had been there 22 years. The other building on the site is the Idwal Cottage Youth Hostel, one of the first to open in 1931.

It began life as the manager's house for the 'Idwal Hone Stone quarry which is immediately behind both buildings. It was built and owned by Lord Penrhyn who also owned one of the largest slate quarries in the world some four miles down the valley above Bethesda. The soft slate quarried here was considered to be the best blade sharpening stone in the world. Soaked in oil it was even used to hone surgeon's scalpels. School writing slates were also produced here.

The old house was initially leased to the YHA for twenty pounds a year until it was finally bought for five thousand pounds in 1963. The wooden building seen in the woods nearby which looks like a battery hen shed is a recent replacement for a similar structure which was originally designed as extra accommodation by the architect Colwyn Foulkes for

Llanfihangel Glyn Myfyr youth hostel up on the Hiraethog moors in 1931. Unfortunately this hostel had to close after a year due to local opposition. The wooden hut was dismantled and brought here in 1932 and has been used ever since until 2018 when a tree fell one stormy night and completely destroyed it; it is still known as 'Foulkes' hut'.

The quarry is first mentioned in 1759 when it apparently closed, only to be re-opened soon after by Lord Penrhyn. A cargo manifest of undressed slate from the quarry is recorded as having been shipped to America in 1796. In 1801 he leased the quarry to a Samuel Worthington and his partners for twenty pounds a year and royalties for a term of twenty one years. The final mention of any note was in 1864 when a Thomas Thomas from Bangor was working the quarry with a workforce of seven men. Its output gradually declined and although intermittent digging continued over the years by individuals (I myself have a piece which I dug out), it has lain dormant for several decades. Today it is sometimes used for wet weather climbing and abseil practise and has been affectionately daubed 'Tin Can Alley' by local climbers. The mature pine trees around the car park were planted to disguise the spoil heaps, and the area around them used for many years as a 'wild camping' site. It was leased by the YHA off the Penrhyn estate for a pound a year until they finally bought it in 1981.

Follow the minor road north through the trees and the little school of Glan Rhyd Idwal can be seen on the left. It was first built in 1853 as an outlying church by Lord Penrhyn but over the years became a school which eventually closed in 1939. Even during its time as a school it still had a small altar and a stone font cut from a rock from the shores of Llyn Ogwen. It received a School Inspector's Report one year which was amongst the best in Wales. For many years it too was leased by the Youth Hostel as an extra dormitory until it was bought in 1986; today, it is the Hostel Manager's private residence.

This road was built by Lord Penrhyn in 1792 and carries an

amusing little story as to why it was built. After losing his Parliamentary seat, due he claimed to the residents of Conwy voting against him he swore he would "make grass grow on the streets of Conwy" and building this road served to take away the traffic from the coastal approach to North Wales. Although he did indeed lose his seat it wasn't until after the road was built!

He went on to continue the road to Capel Curig where, in 1801 he built his hotel, the 'Capel Curig Inn'. This in effect did open up a viable alternative route to the area as it linked up with 'Cernioge Fawr Inn' near Pentrefoelas which supported a coach service and changes of horses.

The first landlord of the Capel Curig Inn, affectionately known as 'Honest Griffiths' was 'mine host' there for many years. Following Queen Victoria's visit in 1870 it was re-named the 'Royal Hotel'; indeed, Edward VII, Edward VIII and George V were all royal visitors in turn. In 1955 the hotel closed and became a mountaineering centre and re-named Plas y Brenin which is still a popular residential base for mountaineering courses and activities.

Cross the cattle grid and admire the opening vista showing the lower valley which is known as Nant Ffrancon. For thousands of years following the Ice Age the valley would have contained a long shallow lake which, over the centuries slowly dried to become a birch and alder swamp. Eventually man straightened the river and drained the valley bottom to produce the grassland we see today. Notice the huge concrete and stone blocks constructed by the Home Guard as part of their 'bit' to stop German tanks, Rommel must have had many a sleepless night worrying about these!

Returning back through the trees and past the snack bar we cross the turbulent little stream which drains Llyn Idwal in a series of foamy cataracts bouncing beneath a photogenic footbridge.

The next building which stands on the junction of Penrhyn's road and the A5 is 'Ogwen Cottage' which was for decades an

Devil's Kitchen

Adventure Centre for Birmingham Education Authority. It started life as a Toll cottage which Telford himself designed and later became a small hotel patronised for many years by climbers who had found Ogwen to be an excellent climbing centre. A tale is told how the first ascent of the fearsome 'Twll Du' or 'Devil's Kitchen' which rears above the top end of Llyn Idwal was made in the terrible winter of 1895 using a coal pick 'borrowed' from Mrs. Jones, Ogwen Cottage! Archer Thompson and Harold Hughes seized their opportunity when they noticed the 'Kitchen' had been half filled with compact snow. Anyone who has ever looked up into this dark, awful cleft or down its thunderous waterfall from above will appreciate that it was no light undertaking. The actual ascent of the rock walls of the 'Kitchen' was not done until 1898.

Interestingly enough the term 'Devil's Kitchen' was first applied to somewhere vaguely in the Ogwen valley by the Liverpool sailors who blamed the sudden squalls which hit them from the mountains. Over time 'Twll Du' has been specifically chosen as the source of these squalls and the name 'Devil's

Kitchen' has stayed. There are other legends concerning the Druids on Anglesey who prayed to their gods for deliverance from the impending Roman invasion and were rewarded by a series of storms from the 'Devil's Kitchen' which at least postponed the Roman assault.

The 'Cottage' was bought in 1959 by Ron James who innovatively set up a climbing school. His Instructors often found themselves rescuing climbers in difficulties on local crags and eventually this service evolved to form the Ogwen Valley Mountain Rescue Team. He sold the 'Cottage' to Birmingham LEA in 1964 and stayed on as Chief Instructor. In 2014 the National Trust bought it, and as well as offering accommodation, they offer adventure courses in conjunction with the Outward Bound movement.

We are now on the A5 and turn left to walk down the pavement towards where the first bridge to cross the river Ogwen stands a mere hundred yards away.

In 1801 the Act of Union between Ireland and Britain came into force; this meant that members of parliament would need to travel from the Emerald Isle to Westminister. The roads in both countries were at the time, pitiful and little more than rough tracks. Indeed, before Penrhyn's 1792 road it is doubtful if any wheeled carriage had ever traversed the valley. The road network in England and Wales were a series of Turnpike roads, the quality of which depended on each individual governing trust. The road between Capel Curig and Bangor was run by the 'Capel Curig Turnpike Trust' which had been formed in 1802.

In 1810 following the Government's decision to build the main Irish port in Holyhead rather than the fiercely contested Porth Dinllaen on the Llyn peninsula Thomas Telford was appointed to improve the road; this was in 1815. Although he used large sections of the existing route he also constructed several miles of new sections by-passing the original course. By 1826, following the completion of his Menai suspension bridge the road was a significant improvement. The trip from London to Holyhead now took 27 hours compared to the previous time of 45 hours. Traditionally the A5 starts at the 'Marble Arch' in London and ends 252 miles later at the 'Admiralty Arch' which was raised in 1821 to commemorate George IV's visit to Holyhead.

Just before reaching the bridge glance over to your left at a level piece of ground between the wall and the river Idwal. This is where the original Ogwen tea shack used to be. It started life as a small green caravan which was towed up daily from Bethesda to sell tea and cakes by a character called Merfyn. Eventually the deteriorating chassis meant it became a permanent fixture and following various improvements and add ons over the years became the Ogwen tea shack loved by three generations. Its boarded front window would open out on to the wall as a counter. In 1982 when the County Council decided to open their own tea bar on the site of the present one the old shack had to be removed with the franchise for running the new one offered as a sweetener to the Bethesda family who owned it.

Rhaeadr y Benglog

Look down off the bridge and see the meeting of the two rivers. The confluence of the Ogwen and the Idwal must be the most foamy, bad tempered union of any two rivers in Wales as they battle their way down a huge slab of rock. This attrition continues for another three waterfalls until, seemingly the Ogwen prevails to retain its name all the way to the sea.

Immediately beneath and parallel to the present road the obvious green lane leading down the valley until it is swallowed by the A5 was the turnpike road. One has to admire the wall and the size of the boulders which still keeps much of the old road from collapsing into the river below. A section did collapse in the winter of 2019 to reveal how much work actually went into its original construction, it also shows the strength of a raging mountain stream.

Several episodes of the 1959 TV programme 'William Tell' were filmed here, a little lower down the valley and on the slopes of Fachwen above the lower end of Llyn Padarn. A little opening in the wall at the far end of the bridge will take you down some rough steps to the old road.

The turnpike roads were never popular, as events in South Wales daubed the 'Rebecca Riots' were to prove when toll gates were destroyed by men disguised as women. There was much recorded vandalism on this road too with several instances of stones being thrown down into the gorge. The coming of the railways and an 1888 act eventually sounded the death knell of the British turnpike roads.

Follow the old road for no more than twenty yards down the valley and pick up a faint track dropping down to the left. This soon develops into a zig zagging track of rough slabs forming steps and it has a history. When Pennant toured Wales in 1778 there were two rough tracks up the Ogwen valley each either side of the river. This descending track joined them and could well be the location he described in his book 'A tour in Wales' :-

Old Smithy

"The worse horse paths in Wales, cut into the rock in the rudest manner of steps"...

At the bottom, near the river a small squat building appears which upon closer inspection has a military look. During the war the Home Guard converted it into a pill box; doubtless another source of worry for Hitler and his Generals. It was built as a Smithy to service the cattle whose drovers had walked from Anglesey and the Llyn on their way to markets such as Shrewsbury. A two piece shoe was needed for cattle whose hoofs are cloven and this is where they were fitted, thus allowing them to cross the mountains. The age of the Drovers also came to an end with the coming of the railways.

The river below has already jumped two of its three waterfalls and has gathered itself in a pool before running for the next jump. Look carefully near the far bank and you will see all that remains of the original bridge in the form of a single slab of rock which has withstood centuries of flood; fair play!

All around you will see raw evidence of the Ice Age. Shining slabs of wet rock catching the sun will show the striation marks made by ice glaciers a thousand feet thick slowly dragging trapped boulders along the bedrock to leave these obvious scratches.

Two hundred yards away not far from the electric pole on the western side of the river there is a spring which was once considered a healing well. I remember the old lady who lived in the nearby farmhouse Blaen Nant describing how women would walk up from Bethesda with bottles to carry some of this water home if a member of the family was unwell.

We must now climb back up to the A5 and pause perhaps on the way to reflect on a sad incident which happened here in 1670. Two drovers, a father and son were returning to Anglesey when they were set upon near this spot by some robbers. They were both killed but the whole incident had been witnessed by a young shepherd and his dog. In his haste to get away he was seen and the murderers chased him. After hiding beneath a rock for hours and holding his dog's nose to prevent it barking he eventually crawled out and ran home to raise the alarm. Meanwhile the robbers had hidden the drovers' bodies and

Reconstructed 19 century bridge

escaped, never to be caught. It was years before their bodies were found deep in a rocky cleft near the waterfalls; they were buried in Llanllechid churchyard.

Back at the A5 cross the road and climb over a slate stile in memory of Alf Embleton, a worthy from the world of walking who was a Treasurer of the Rambler's Association and instrumental in acquiring the Idwal Youth Hostel nearby; he died in 1961.

Down on the right unless the river is prohibitively high you can scramble down to inspect the re-constructed skeletal bridge hiding beneath the A5. This was where the old toll or turnpike road crossed and is structurally safe to venture on. Looking up at the underbelly of Telford's bridge you can see the join where the bridge was widened in the 1930s, the calcite deposits are significantly heavier on his 1815 arch. The remains of a few anchors driven into the rocks near the river bed can also be seen where the original scaffolding was secured.

Continue along the rough path through the extensive boulder field, negotiating at one point the absence of a small footbridge as you make your way towards the lake. Here somewhere amongst these huge boulders is a cave called 'Ogof Ifan Bach'. Whoever he was or why he had a cave named after him is not recorded, but then, hasn't every cave in Wales been

Spent bullets

attributed a legend or person of note? Rhys Goch Eryri who supported Owain Glyndwr when he had to go into hiding is also reputed to have hidden in a cave somewhere on these slopes.

The small dam which holds back the lake is only two feet high and was built in the first decade of last century by the Penrhyn estate to increase the volume of the lake. Water was a precious commodity for his industrial enterprises in the Ogwen Valley. A keen angler, he introduced 'Loch Leven' trout into Llyn Ogwen as well as some of the other lakes in the cwms above. The lake itself which is nowhere deeper than ten feet is now managed by the Ogwen Valley Fishing Association.

The path which was one of the two Pennant described continues through the rocks forming the lower slopes of Pen yr Ole Wen, one of Wales' three thousand foot mountains. If you have time and patience to wander 'off piste' look amongst these rocks you will find spent bullets, shards of shrapnel, and even the tail fins of mortar bombs, relics of the last war when troops were brought here for training.

Ahead is another remnant of the war, a pill box similar in construction to the old adapted Smithy at the foot of the Benglog falls. Today, it is the abode of sheep (and their droppings!) or the occasional camper. The slopes now open out a little but are no less rocky as you continue parallel to the lake.

Some three hundred yards before the alluvial shallows formed by the Lloer and Dena streams at the head of the lake a conspicuous boulder perched on the bedrock catches your eye, it is half way between the path and the lake. This is one of only two true 'rocking stones' I know of in Snowdonia; the other being high up in Cwm Perfedd above Nant Ffrancon. There are several of these glacially carried 'perched blocks' which have been called 'rocking stones' but in reality if they ever did rock too much human attention have ruined their rocking properties, or, too little in dense fir plantations where falling leaves become soil have locked them into immobility.

We soon cross the river Lloer where, if you glance across

Rocking Stone

the lake, Tryfan's best profile is revealed as it dramatically rises to a pointed triangle of three thousand and ten feet; the lowest of our fifteen giants! It is the only peak whose summit cannot be reached without the use of the hands. I tried once, and a clear day will reveal two ten foot monoliths on the very top called 'Adam' and 'Eve' and show the reason I failed! One season in the mid sixties several sightings of a white mouse were reported on the summit which seemed to live off crumbs and other offerings left by climbers. Neither the mouse nor its offspring have been seen for years, but the seagulls will still clear away abandoned edibles apart from orange and banana skins. Why do people still desecrate places that requires such effort to get there?

By following the signposted path behind the farm of 'Tal-y-Llyn Ogwen' and picking up the track we arrive once again on the A5. Opposite the old Penrhyn road still continues as a rough track south and parallel to the A5 to Capel Curig to emerge in four miles behind the shop and post office. The original road continued west and emerged opposite the Capel Curig Inn itself.

We now turn right and walk back towards the lake along the A5.

According to an old Welsh poem which describes the burial sites of ancient British warriors, Bedivere, one of Arthur's knights is buried somewhere on the rugged slopes of Tryfan.

Also buried on Tryfan in a hidden cave is a horde of treasure left by one of the many Irish tribes who occupied parts of Wales following the Roman departure. Many were invaders from Scandinavia who had settled in Ireland. Folklore tells of a chieftain called Cunedda from the Scottish borders who came down with his army to conquer and repulse these tribes who had settled here for three generations. The Irish left having hidden their treasure fully intending to return! Another similar tribe had settled in Nant Gwynant before a telling battle also forced them to flee.

A young shepherd once stumbled across the cave whilst looking for a lost sheep and was amazed to find such riches, he decided to fetch his brother who was nearby also searching for the sheep to help carry the treasure. When they returned, as in many such tales he couldn't find the cave entrance. Another version tells of a huge black dog which guards the treasure. Tradition dictates it will be an Irishman who will eventually find the cave and claim its treasure!

The large boulder field of huge stones protruding into the lake is called 'Y Penrhyn Melyn' but known locally as 'Y 'Foty' after a dwelling which once stood here. 'Foty is an abbreviated version of 'Hafod-ty' meaning summer dwelling. It was from amongst these boulders that the font for Glan Rhyd Idwal school/church came.

The old turnpike road passed on the very shore between the rocks and the lake. The remains of the road can be followed past the ruins of 'Foty tucked on the left below the A5 which was used for many years as a fishing hut. It must have been quite a sight to see a post chaise with two horses emerging from around these rocks with a full gale blowing waves and spume across the track! At the western end of the 'Foty a small causeway carried the old turnpike road across a tongue of water, its remains can still be seen. The boulder field has also been cited as another spot where the crock of Irish treasure is hidden.

For many years the 'Foty was considered to be haunted and locals would keep well clear after dark. One version maintains it to be a man wearing a silk hat who could disappear in a ring of fire. Another oft told tale describes how an empty coach to Capel Curig picked up a passanger one evening just as it was getting dark. Almost immediately the horses became agitated and although the four miles to Capel Curig is mostly downhill they struggled to pull the coach as if it had something extremely heavy in it. By the time they arrived at the Capel Curig Inn they were covered in lather. When the driver stopped his passenger vanished leaving a sickly smell of sulphur and brimstone which hung in the air for ages; he was convinced to his dying day that he had carried the Devil himself that night!

Immediately to the south rising up in a series of buttresses, gullies and scree is the north ridge of Tryfan, which offers a splendid scramble up the mountain's spur. The lowest of these buttresses which was carved over thousands of years into a slightly steeper crag by the slow moving glacier has for decades been used for rock climbing. Having been adopted by

The painted V on the milestone Buttress

generations of climbers it bears the English name of 'Milestone Buttress' after Telford's tenth milestone from Bangor which once stood beneath it. Sometime in the early 70s the milestone was stolen but in the climbing world and even on OS maps the name remains.

If you look carefully at the highest point of the cliff you will see a very faint V painted on the rock. This was done during the enthusiastic celebrations which erupted everywhere when the war ended. Worn smooth by decades of nailed boots the routes on the 'Milestone Buttress' are mainly for novices and hardly a dry day passes when the crag is not covered in colourful figures, many dry mouthed youngsters have had their characters developed here by enthusiastic young Instructors!

Half a mile away the lower end of the lake and the little cluster of trees marks the end of this upper valley before a set of three waterfalls plunges down a rock step. 'Y Benglog' is the name given to this steep rock step which rises abruptly from the lower valley called 'Nant Ffrancon'; a dramatic climb of three

Gyrating Water Spouts

hundred feet in less than a quarter of a mile. Then, on the very lip of this rock step is Llyn Ogwen just on the point when the valley suddenly turns east; a topography which can produce an interesting phenomenon. There have been several occasions in blustery winds when I have sat in the car by the 'Foty with my camera waiting for the perfect photo. The wind which blows up the lower valley is suddenly pushed up by the rock step and bounces off the lower slopes of 'Y Garn' a full 80 degrees along its new easterly direction. This sometimes causes dramatic mini whirlwinds and gyrating water spouts to dance demonically across the surface of the lake and well worth investing a spare half hour to wait and watch!

The last feature worth mentioning just before arriving back at the snack bar for a deserved cuppa is the little stream tumbling down on your left from 'Llyn Bochlwyd' which lies in the very bosom of 'Tryfan' and 'Glyder Fach'. For its size and length it must be one of the most turbulent little streams in Snowdonia; as it drops 800 feet in less than half a mile. In 12,000 years it has surely carried several tons of 'Tryfan' and 'Glyder Fach' to form the alluvial fan spreading into the lake. It was from here, safely away from the road that many of the rounds littering the rocks across the lake were fired by the soldiers training for D Day.

A couple of hundred yards is now all that remains back to the car.

So, summing up; 'Y Benglog' has an attractive roadside lake fed by five of Wales' twenty 2,000 foot lakes and is surrounded by six out of the fifteen Weish 3,000 peaks. It has tradition, history, folklore, the occasional weather phenomenon, a few waterfalls and even a couple of ghosts! You might even stumble across some Irish treasure! Oh, and you can even buy a cup of tea and a currant square in a friendly tea shack which is managed by the third generation of the same local family! so why wouldn't you want to spend half a day exploring the 'Benglog'?

Chapter 7

The Welsh Tsunami and a lost town

In this chapter I sneak a glance at the changing coastline of Wales and the way folk memory have relied on legends to make sense of some of these changes. Other changes which occurred within recorded history as a result of specific events are more verifiable and serve to show just how fragile and temporary our coastline really is.

Early depiction of the floods

Most Welsh schoolchildren have grown up knowing the legend of Cantref Gwaelod. They have heard how Seithennin, the guardian of the sea wall, forgot to shut the floodgates one night because he was drunk, and how, as a result hundreds of acres of land belonging to the chieftain Gwyddno Garanhir were lost to the sea of Cardigan Bay forever. A small consolation is being able to hear the bells of the drowned churches tolling beneath the waves just out from the coastal town of Aberdyfi on quiet evenings. Don't the tree stumps which are revealed at low water on the sands of Ynys Las, Borth only serve to prove the legend? And aren't the causeways Sarn Badrig, Sarn Bwch, and Sarn Gynfelyn which can be seen extending in straight lines far out into Cardigan Bay further evidence of ruined sea walls? There is little doubt that these lands were inhabited 7,000 years ago. One school of thought believes two events, one at 4,000 BC and 1,500 BC respectively were chiefly responsible for the inundation of Cantref Gwaelod. Reference to this lost land is made in the Black Book of Carmarthen.

A similar fate occurred in Conway Bay in the sixth century when Helig ap Glannawg lost a large tract of his kingdom to the hungry sea. According to local fishermen the rectangular outline of his palace Llys Helig can be seen when the sea is calm a mile out from Dwygyfylchi at low tide. Two miles west the extensive Lavan sands easily noticed from the A55, is an area which was

8,000 year old tree stumps

Sarn Cynfelyn

apparently marshland containing a handful of houses up to the seventh century before it too was lost to the sea. Even the rocky knoll where Caer Arianrhod of the Mabinogion tales once stood is revealed as a reef in low Spring tides on the northern coast of Llyn. Even older than these floodings was a land known as Teithi Hen's kingdom between St. David's and Ireland out in St. George's Channel. Legend has the ruler Teithi only just managing to escape the floodwaters on his horse.

The legends slowly mutated to infer that these were sudden deluges and a result of God's wrath because the people led sinful lives. In the seventeenth century even some of Wales' lakes jumped on this particular bandwagon of myths as in the case of Tegid, Llynclys, Llyn Llech Owen and Syfaddan. Finishing touches like floating harps, cradles or gloves found after the event were added as the stories became consolidated into their much told forms. The tolling bells appeared in the nineteenth century.

Wales would indeed be the poorer without her legends, the best of which are delicately poised between credulity and fantasy. One characteristic of these folk memory stories is their ability to remember names, characters and events but to lose the context and perspective of time as they become compressed into legends.

However, although losing these coastal lands to the sea was very real, the actual process was altogether more gradual, most of which occurred in the few thousand years following the Ice Age which effectively ended 12,000 years ago. The pebble strewn causeways of Sarn Cynfelyn, Sarn Bwch and Sarn Badrig which run in straight lines out into Cardigan bay were first cited as ruined sea walls by the scholar Robert Vaughan of Hengwrt and his contemporaries but they have been subsequently shown to be natural geological features and glacial till.

For the Cantref Gwaelod legend in its most lurid form to be true it would have taken a sea level rise of 120 feet. Even the more moderate version in the 'Black Book of Carmarthen' would have needed a 60 foot rise. We know the Romans experienced difficulty crossing to Anglesey across the Menai Strait almost 2,000 years ago. Bearing in mind the Strait have a maximum depth of thirty feet, for the Llys Helig legend to be true the required rise of forty would have meant the Romans could have walked across at the time of their invasion. Clearly this was not so.

The Irish Sea Icefield covered most of Britain apart from Southern England. As this Icefield melted the sea levels rose slightly, an important factor in the process. But so too the colossal weight of the ice which had been pressing the Northern landmass of Britain for over two million years was lifted causing a slow but steady raising of the land, this resulted in the many raised beaches on the west coast of Scotland. This see saw action had the opposite effect on Southern Britain as the land slowly tilted back down to pre-glacial levels. It is estimated that since Roman times the sea level in Southern Wales has risen 15 feet; or the land has dropped 15 feet. This and natural erosion powered by occasional significant storms has ensured that Wales, and indeed Britain is still slowly shrinking albeit it at different rates in different areas.

There is a gravestone in Abergele churchyard which claims its occupant once lived 3 miles to the north in what is today open sea. Many will still remember when the sea wall in Towyn on the North Wales coast was overwhelmed in 1990 due to a particularly high tide and strong winds which resulted in a storm surge. Modern technology and machinery managed to repair the damage which was only a modest breach in the overall context of sea flooding, but a similar event a few centuries ago in the age of picks and shovels would doubtless have triggered more legends about how the lost lands of Towyn and Pensarn were swallowed by the hungry sea.

So, although these floodings which form the basis of so many legends were far more gradual than their stories suggest there are two incidents which occurred on the southern shores of Wales which when measured on the geological clock were very much sudden, cataclysmic events.

The first I shall describe happened at 9.00am on the 20th January 1606. There had been a south westerly borne storm of some magnitude for three days and the low lying land near Newport was already saturated with rainwater. The Severn estuary has the second highest tide in the world and on that fateful morning there was a Spring tide driven by the gale. The difference between high and low water in a Spring tide here is 40 feet (as opposed to 21 feet in Neap tides). There was also a report that an earthquake had been felt far out to sea. The elements had seemingly conspired to produce what was to become a major disaster, to coin a modern phrase, a perfect storm was about to break. A contemporary report describes what was seen from the high ground at Mumbles :-

"The deluge was something awful to behold, people who stood in the hillside saw far out to sea, huge and mighty hills of water tumbling one over each other in such sort and confusion as if the greatest mountains of the world were rolling forward to overwhelm the land. Forward rushed the maddened waters of the Atlantic, and in the course of a few moments the great tidal wall of sea completely overwhelmed the flat marshy lands and plains around the coast,

destroying farmsteads and villages ... and literally wiping out of existence the ancient farms and meadow lands which had baffled the sea from immemorial time".

Although not on the scale of the 2004 Boxing Day Tsunami in the Indian Ocean it is estimated 2,000 people died during the event and in the aftermath. Twenty six parishes between Mathern and Rumney were swamped as an area of coast twenty four miles long was flooded up to four miles inland. Swansea, Cardiff and Newport were swamped and St. Mary's church in Newport was washed away. An old graveyard belonging to St. Thomas' church in Swansea was destroyed leaving bodies and coffins spread asunder. The ancient track servicing Penrice castle on the Gower totally disappeared and many thousands of livestock were lost. Across the channel in Burnham floods up to twelve feet deep were reported as surely the largest Severn Bore in history surged its terrible way inland.

To understand why this was so severe one has to look at the geography of the area affected. The coastal plains lying to the east of Newport are known as the Caldicot and Wentlog levels. The area is also generally referred to as the 'Moor'. The land is very low and without doubt if it wasn't for the sea defences which have existed in some form for nearly two thousand years it would have been lost to the sea.

The Romans had attempted to drain the land and had built an embankment which was later developed by the Monks of Goldcliff Priory which is known as the 'Monk's Ditch'. At one point this impressive dyke carries water seawards a full eight feet above the level of the surrounding fields. These drainage dykes are known locally as 'reens'. Many of these 'reens' carry colourful names like 'Hare's Reen', 'Cock Street Reen', 'Oxleaze Reen' and 'Ynys Mead Reen'. A glance at the OS map will show just how flat this land is and just how many of these reens are needed. The area was therefore ripe for the ensuing chaos that a Tsunami of that magnitude would bring.

Redwick church

As with all such floods there were tales of rescue and miraculous escapes. Local gentry Sir Walter Montague and Lord Herbert sent out several boats which saved many dozens as people clung to the few trees and surviving buildings. There is one story describing a mother hurriedly placing her partially clothed young daughter high up on the beam of their home as the terrible waters approached. When found, hours later the little girl had managed to keep warm by cuddling a chicken which had also taken refuge on the beam!

Several of the local churches which survived have the height of this 1606 flood marked high up on their walls. St. Mary's church in Nash which is known as the 'Cathedral of the Moor' has the flood marked on the North East buttress. St. Peterstone church, St. Brides not only has the flood height marked but the tower is still leaning slightly as a result of the incident. The church was originally built by Mabel, wife of the earl of Gloucester in 1142 and had to be extensively re-built following Glyndwr's visit in 1404. Today Peterstone church is a private residence.

There is a stone dial on the right of the entrance to St. Thomas' church, Redwick (which has one of the few remaining rood screens and lofts in Gwent) installed in the porch marking the height of the floodwater. The church was known as St. Michael the Archangel in the sixteenth century, by the nineteenth century it had been changed to St. Mary's and then in the 1870s it was given its present designation. It too was all but destroyed by Glyndwr; heavily vandalized by Cromwell and even had its bell tower damaged by the Luftwaffe who dropped three bombs in the nearby field. St. Tewdric's church in Mathern was also damaged in this terrible event. The old church was named after Tewdric, the sixth century king of Glamorgan who died of his wounds following the battle of Tintern against the Saxons. The nearby palace which also survived the flood was once the residence of William Morgan whose translation of the bible in 1588 did as much as anyone to preserve the Welsh language.

It wasn't until 1607 that London newspapers covered the story adopting the view that God may have used the flood to punish the sinful; that old chestnut!

Tablet at Redwick church

The second coastal inundation that I shall describe was not a sudden event like the 1606 Tsunami, although in the geological time scale, perhaps it was. Rather it was a series of storms over perhaps a hundred and eighty years which saw one of the most important towns in the area disappear completely.

How many of the thousands of drivers travelling along the M4 between Swansea and Port Talbot I wonder realize that they are driving over part of the ancient town of Kenfig which was lost to a series of devastating sand storms almost six centuries ago?

The town of Kenfig was one of the most important coastal settlements in the area. It had easy access to the sea along the river Kenfig and was tokenly defended by a castle. The Norman, Robert Fitzhamon had established a maritime trading centre here in 1100 as one of the early priorities of the Norman incursion into Wales. The castle had been completed by 1185.

The old manuscript 'Brut y Tywysogion' records that "Khynffig" was attacked by the Danes in 893. In 1185 the town was burnt in the Welsh revolt. Llywelyn Fawr is also known to have attacked Kenfig in 1230. By 1397 its importance as a strategic trading port and English foothold had long been established when it received its own Charter to become a recognized town. In hindsight however, the writing was already on the wall; Kenfig was doomed.

In 1405 Kenfig castle hosted its penultimate battle when Owain Glyndwr attacked. But, ironically, the castle's final battle would be a losing one against the encroaching sand whose advance was inexorable. Two huge storms in 1246 and 1249 respectively demonstrated what nature had in mind for Kenfig as large tracts of land and several dwellings were left covered in sand. Another major sand storm is recorded in 1317 and by 1344 rent for large areas of land could not be collected as they had effectively become sand dunes. Old manuscripts show the Monks of Margam had to give a substantial rent rebate for a tenement of land known as the 'Addelers' in 1478. The sea played its part in all this as winter storms brought more sand as fodder

Traeth Lavan

for the south westerly gales. In 1485 a new church was built in nearby Pyle to replace the church in Kenfig which had finally lost its battle against the sand.

John Leland visited in 1539 and alludes to the sand which was slowly devouring the old town. It seems the three day storm of 1606 was the final death knell for Kenfig when sand of biblical proportions was blown in by the south westerly gales as the town to all purpose was abandoned. A report in 1660 describes most of the town to be covered in sand and by 1676 the river had been completely clogged up; no boat of any significant size would ever reach the castle again. Radio carbon dating have confirmed that Kenfig has been a settlement for 4,000 years, and in eighteen decades it had become 1600 acres of sand dunes.

The salt marsh of Oxwich was also created by the incursion of sand as the river which once serviced Penrice castle was cut off from the sea. The demise of Pennard church came about due to sand and coastal flooding in 1430, two further examples of the South Wales coast losing its battle against the sea.

Further north in Gwynedd, the little church of Llandanwg nestling just to the south of Harlech needs the occasional removal of several tons of sand by local volunteers following gales. At one time this was a stopping off point for corpses on their way to be buried on Bardsey Island.

A modern example of this losing battle against the sea is the little village of Fairbourne hugging the southern shore of the Mawddach estuary opposite Barmouth. Gwynedd council have declared that no work would be done to the sea defences after 2054 due to the projected rise in sea levels. The little village was created by Solomon Andrews as a holiday project in 1865 and then later bought by the flour maker Sir Arthur McDougall. Gwynedd's policy does to house prices in Fairbourne what Herod did to child minding.

All rules have exceptions and there are several examples where the sea has seemingly retreated due to silting and long shore drifting. One only has to look at the castles of Beamaris, Harlech and Flint to see evidence of this. Indeed, it could be argued that Kenfig's demise ironically came about as a result of the sea losing ground to the land.

Today all that remains of Kenfig is one corner of the castle ruins and the 70 acre Kenfig Pool where, I am told, if you listen on a quiet evening the bells of the old church might still be heard!

Kenfig pool   Llun: Wiki commons

Chapter 8

A Cambrian Manhunt!

This is a story from the life I led before becoming a teacher; when the hours were long, the work hard and the income uncertain. The perks however was being outdoors conducting a variety of adventures which were held together by a lot of fun. This was one such weekend.

A now dilapidated Anchor Inn

The idea was simple, cross the 40 mile waist of Wales in two days and avoid capture! Getting someone to pay for the privilege was a little more complicated; but do-able. At the time I ran an Outdoor Pursuit Centre in Snowdonia and was constantly looking for fresh ideas and schemes to offer paying members of the public.

And so, after some provocative advertising in an Outdoor magazine challenging any group who fancied their chances, a number of groups were booked for a series of such events for the Summer. Several took place in Snowdonia and three which includes this one took place in Mid Wales.

I'd arranged to meet this particular group at the Anchor Inn on the Welsh/English border at 7.00pm on a Friday evening. They were a group of venture scouts attending college from the Midlands. My highly trained search squad comprised of my brother 'Dash' and myself. Other staff members were my father who lived in the area and whose telephone number was given for emergencies, and Ted.

The rules were simple. There would be four tasks to complete at specific locations and set times and the group would be 'immune' from capture an hour either side of these tasks! There would also be immunity for twelve hours from 7.00pm Saturday when we would all meet at a pre arranged camp. Once they'd signed the indemnity forms (yes, even in the early 80s!) and settled the balance of the fee (why else would I be there?) we checked their safety equipment; map, compass, waterproofs, sleeping bag, first aid kit, and basic rations and gave them their final instructions. I then set them off with an hour's start. It never failed to amuse me how every group would begin their forty mile trek with a sprint! It was 7.45 and they had two hours of daylight. We finished our pints and leisurely made our way to my father's house; there would be no hunting that night!

Almost the whole of Mid Wales is a sparsely populated area mainly comprising of everything which is rural. The area is defined by the countless small wooded valleys, winding between

Our 'hunting chariot'

bleak rounded hills, themselves often covered in forestry plantations, beautiful and remote but an absolute nightmare if you can't read a map! For this reason we had to keep more of an eye on them than they realized.

The first task they had to complete the following morning was an easy one which deliberately didn't need supervision, and they had until 11.00 to complete it. They could potentially have pushed on through the night, and completed the task before resting up, I wanted to give them the scope to do this. The second task however would be supervised, giving me the opportunity to check on their wellbeing. For this first task they had to place a dummy explosive charge under a footbridge crossing a stream; this sophisticated piece of kit was a small teddy bear – 'Ted'; the fourth member of staff, or to give him his full title 'Superted'!

We settled in the bracken with our binoculars like a couple

of deer stalkers overlooking the bridge about half a mile away, sending out positive thoughts to deter any potential sheep tics which might decide to attach themselves on us and waited. We had no intention of 'catching' them at this early stage, merely get an idea of their location and route schedule if possible. Impressively we didn't spot them until they were hurrying away from the bridge, having completed their task; it was 10.30 am, they were taking it very seriously!

We watched them safely out of sight and ambled down to retrieve Ted.

The intrepid group of four had just under five hours to make the next checkpoint which as the crow flies was only 8 miles away. In reality there were several hills and valleys with two streams and a river, there were also some minor roads depending on which route they took before a network of tracks would lead them through the forest to the designated spot.

The small footbridge

The next task was set in small glade in Dol-gau forest in the hills above the village of Staylittle and was scheduled for 3.00pm. It was an electric fence compound comprising of four hurdles some eight foot square. We would raise each corner with four additional poles and attach a live agricultural electric wire at a height of six foot. Using ropes and lengths of timber provided, their task was to get one of the group inside and rescue a hostage tied to a stake in the middle; yes! you've guessed it – the long suffering Ted! Again we had no intention of effecting a 'capture' at this stage unless they made it too easy. So once we'd set the 'electrified compound' up we patrolled the obvious forest track approaches, the noise of our land rover giving them ample opportunity to leap into the trees if they were naïve enough to approach using the tracks. We didn't spot them until they were well inside their immunity time; they were good.

When they arrived and were enjoying the coffee we'd prepared they had a 'wink, wink, nudge, nudge' style confession how they were nearly caught crossing the road by a red bricked cottage some two hours earlier, and asked...

"Did you have anyone there?"

I took a stab in the dark and confessed "If it was a land rover with a fellow wearing a cloth cap he was one of us"

"Yes, it was!"

"Well you did have a close shave then! Well done for getting through!"

That left them convinced that anyone with a cloth cap and a land rover was one of our battalion of dedicated searchers; it also described 90% of the farmers in Mid Wales!

Anyone who has knowingly touched a farm electric fence powered by a twelve volt leisure battery will know the anticipation is worse than the actual shock it gives; such was the case here.

Fair play; they very quickly grasped what was required and within twenty minutes had constructed a bridge scaffold and a rudimentary pair of tongs that their 'chosen one' could carry to reach down into the compound. A penknife tied on on one leg of the prongs was for cutting Ted's bonds!

The scaffold was good but they should have checked the knots!

The climb up and across went well despite some alarming creaking and much 'give' in the flexible structure. Reaching down and rescuing Ted (including the stake!) also went according to plan and the chosen one was on course for a successful outcome until he decided to jettison the tongs on the return leg. As he hurled it clear the force proved too much for one corner joint which slipped down about ten inches due to a loose knot. He put out his hand to steady himself and started yelping before he even touched the wire! It was so comical we were all in tucks! The sagging bridge was quickly bolstered by the rest of his laughing friends and he reached terra firma safely and could then see the funny side himself!

Whilst they hurried away using their hour's start we dismantled the compound. We had three hours before they were due at camp and we thought we'd have some fun.

We decided to go where they would see us 'searching' and allow them to 'slip through' the massive cloth capped cordon of their imagination; time enough to 'catch' them tomorrow if we wanted.

So, parking the land rover at a prominent viewpoint overlooking the Twymyn gorge we sort of patrolled the immediate skyline above the road making their obvious choice an unclassified track in the next valley. It worked a treat as they sauntered into camp right on time feeling very pleased with themselves having evaded capture and more than half way across Wales.

We'd set up camp near the old lead mines of Dylife which has, four hundred yards away the Star Inn, the highest pub above sea level in Wales. It was an enjoyable evening, playing pool and chatting and they turned out to be a very nice group of young men.

Next morning slightly less than bright eyed and bushy tailed they set off, funnily enough without sprinting whilst we too lethargically broke camp.

The next task was set in a semi ruined barn at the confluence of two streams high up the Clywedog valley on the very shoulder of the Pumlumon plateau. Using a set of complicated instructions in jig-saw form they had to decide which one of five boxes they had to open to release Ted. The boxes, attached to a plank were set upright like miniature wardrobes on a low wall with each 'door' a different colour!

THE DOOR NEXT TO THE RED ONE WILL NOT RELEASE TED
THE CORRECT DOOR IS NEXT TO A PRIMARY COLOUR
TED'S DOOR IS TWO AWAY FROM A RAINBOW COLOUR
A TRAFFIC LIGHT COLOUR IS NEXT TO TED

Piecing together the jig-saw

... are examples of the eight pieces of information they could use once they'd assembled the jig-saw! There was also a timer with a loud buzzer giving them a maximum of fifteen minutes to complete the operation. Each wrong door had a mousetrap and a small tray of dye which would be set off upon opening the door. Oh...and in the correct box Ted was also attached to a booby trap...it was all very dastardly!

They arrived ten minutes early and were glad of a cup of coffee before tackling their next challenge. They had travelled up partly along the old Machynlleth stage road past the site of an ancient gallows and listened with interest as I related the story of John the Blacksmith.

Once again they impressed us as they worked out with a minute to spare which was the correct door, they duly opened it and proceeded to remove Ted only to forget about the booby trap. The small thread which they should have seen wrapped around poor Ted's ankle was attached to the base plate of the mousetrap and in an instant a hand and part of a sleeve was covered in the blue dye which wasn't going to come off for days!

We were high up on the Cambrian moorlands, desolate and featureless apart from the straight edged boundaries of the forestry and a few isolated lakes. They had one task to complete and then it would be downhill all the way to the coast.

We'd already decided not to 'capture' them; they were a game group, young, earnest and a nice bunch; it would mean so much for them to evade us.

Again we chose an obvious skyline to patrol, giving them plenty of warning of our presence. We left the land rover parked by the old abandoned farmhouse of Bugeilyn and walked along the knoll above. We actually spotted one of them as they left the Llwyn-y-gog forest and skirted along the edge of a small ridge bent double making for a shallow stream, they had obviously seen us!

When they re-appeared half an hour later boldly striding towards the designated checkpoint they were within their immunity time and obviously feeling empowered and pleased with themselves.

Meanwhile Ted had been marooned on a small island on Cwm Byr lake some twenty yards offshore and needed rescuing. The means of his rescue would be by raft made using the same timber and ropes used for the electric compound task as well as eight plastic drums. It was a group task to build the raft but only one had to go across, we provided a wet suit and life jacket. For the first time a slight chord of disharmony crept into the group as they debated two different methods of attaching the drums to the raft; the knot tier of the electric compound task wisely kept quiet! Eventually a raft was created and baptised 'Tie-panic'! It wasn't the sleekest, most elegant I've ever seen but it floated and lying on his stomach their chosen champion successfully paddled across and brought the marooned castaway back safely. The relief on Ted's face was almost as obvious as Dash's, whose turn it would have been to retrieve Ted had the group failed!

The island

The 'Tie-panic'

A final hot brew and they were off on their final leg, this time with a little more spring in their steps, most of the route would be downhill. We shouted as they left how we would "definitely get them this time!"

The final rendevouz was to be in the Black Lion inn at Derwen-lâs some four hundred metres away from the highest point of the tide making it an official waist of Wales crossing. Their lift home would be there too.

There was a multitude of route choice from Bugeilyn, two or three long valleys filled with deciduous trees each with a stream and served by several country lanes were the obvious ones. Footpaths linked each valley and until the final three mile approach they could have chosen any one of the canopied corridors. In truth it would have been the hardest section of all if we genuinely wanted to catch them.

Ted was glad to sleep in the back of the land rover while we stopped at Machynlleth for a late lunch containing more than the recommended dose of cholesterol.

We then drove up one of the wooded valleys and down

another stopping by the side of a beautiful bubbling brook. It was a gorgeous setting and with the sun occasionally breaking through the dappled leaves; every shade of green in every paintbox ever made was present. A land rover passed with a cloth capped driver, we looked at each other and laughed!

By 6.30 pm we were in the bar of the Black Lion chatting to one of their fathers; their chauffeur home. We told him how well they'd done and described the tasks they'd had to complete and were told in return how much they had looked forward to the weekend. The group arrived a few minutes after 7.30 tired, soggy and bedraggled but striding with the air of allied POWs reaching the Swiss border in 1943! They had more tales of close shaves, how they'd spotted us searching and how one of our searchers had actually chased them with his dog! Hmm!

It had been a good weekend all round; they had succeeded in crossing the 'Waist of Wales' chased by a multitude of hunters without being captured and we were equally content to have

Black Lion, Derwenlas

spent some time with our Dad, enjoyed a few magical locations in Mid Wales and earned some money whilst doing it! No bear was harmed in the running of this event and Ted's participation in being tied under a footbridge, incarcerated in an electric fence compound, locked in a box with a mousetrap and marooned on an island was entirely voluntary!

A now retired 'Ted'!

I ran several similar courses that Summer but this group stood out. They had asked for a similar challenge later in the Autumn to which I agreed.

I didn't hear anything for eight months and then received a very sad letter explaining that two of them had been killed in a road accident. I was so glad that we had decided not to capture them.

Chapter 9

Animal Memorials

My first experience of a funeral and the concept of loss was the burial of my goldfish in our back garden when I must have been about four. In an ideal world this ritual which is part of the process for dealing with grief is the way children are introduced to bereavement. When animals become pets there is a sort of obligation for  a funeral and quite often there is an accompanying tale which needs to be told.

Tyger's memorial

A few winters ago whilst I was cycling through one of the Hiraethog forests I came across something quite interesting. It was a chilly day, cold enough to see my breath as I panted steadily up a steep forest track keeping an eye out for somewhere suitable to stop and eat my sandwiches. And then, just on the brow of the hill where the track dropped and curved to the right a fire break went off to the left with a patch of sheep nibbled grass between the verge and a luxuriant growth of heather and bilberry; perfect.

It was whilst I was eating my banana, walking around my grass patch to stay warm that I spotted something which seemed out of place in the deeper heather at the fringe of the trees. I pushed through the downy white wetness which was festooned with necklaced spider webs and found it was an upright wooden post covered in grey lichen with writing on it.

Julian's memorial

'JULIAN 14th APRIL 1993 – DIED OF LONELINESS'

How sad! Was it a memorial or a grave?

A horse perhaps who had lost a stable partner?

Could it have been a dog whose favourite walk was along this track until its owner passed away, and it too had pined and succumbed to a broken heart. It was a touching moment of searching contemplation as I wondered about the source of this loneliness and it reminded

Plas y Mynydd

me of another bike ride in the more desolate forests of Mid Wales a couple of years before.

During an altogether longer trip with my brother, we had come upon an old fishing lodge on the shores of a little lake called Llyn Newydd in the upland wilderness south of Machynlleth. Plas y Mynydd or Angler's Retreat was an old wooden tiled cabin dating from 1869 which had been modestly renovated in 1982 following a fire. Originally it was a larger two floored structure which was replaced in the 1950s with an altogether smaller structure.

Nearby, on a little knoll was a row of small graves, they had been there for quite some time and were much neglected. Some words could be made out, 'brave' 'faithful' and 'most patient'; the easiest names which could be read were 'Forbar' and 'Folly'. Graves perhaps of strong, ferocious hunting hounds whose one role in life was to run their quarries down in an all day, relentless baying pursuit. Normally kept in caged packs and

Garneddwen pet cemetery

mass fed these four had obviously crossed the line between being working killers and affectionate pets. Perched as they were on that little mound in such a lonely location I like to think that on dark windy nights their spirits still run over these desolate slopes as tireless as when they were the scourge and nightmare of any fox daring to roam the Cambrian mountains.

Whilst remembering these two encounters I thought of other animal graves I'd stumbled across over the years. Garneddwen animal cemetery on the lower slopes of Aran Benllyn just off the Bala – Dolgellau road was opened in 1968 and called 'The Rest Garden of St. Francis of Assisi'. The little cemetery is no longer used but the dozen or so abandoned graves can still be seen scattered around the remains of an orchard. Many stand askew and broken, the lettering faded and clothed in lichen and moss or propped against a nearby fence, still just about existing. Several pets who had died the previous century had obviously been moved here to be re-buried including the dog shot by his master for worrying sheep. There are also horses, cats, and a bird and all would have paid the then fee of £20.

I recently visited the site and was told by the owner of his intention to raise the stones and use them as a facing for a small reservoir he intends constructing nearby. The earliest I could find was 1885.

There is a row of neatly kept animal graves in Wepre Park, Connah's Quay which also alludes to a dog shot for sheep worrying whose epitaph includes more than a hint of humour. RECTOR – Shot 1890 "Ate without stint, lamb without mint".

Nearby is MORGAN – 1889 "Slow mover, run over".

Also sharing this peaceful spot is VIC – "Had a fit, died quick"

The largest pet cemetery in Europe lies within sight of the A55 expressway in Brynford above the town of Holywell. It opened in 1990 and has between 500 – 600 graves and reportedly conducts up to 3,000 cremations a year. It also has a café where one can shed a quiet tear over a coffee ... and a kit kat perhaps! Sections exclusively for horses are set aside and

Brynford pet cemetery

amongst the more unusual tenants are sparrows, goldfish, alpacas and a 37 year old monkey! On a recent visit the owner enthusiastically described an ongoing project he hopes will bear fruit in the near future; he has set aside a section for dogs of valour who have proved themselves during times of conflict. One example he cited was 'Judy' who was designated an official POW in Sumatra to prevent her being eaten! There is even a section for humans who wish their ashes to be buried with their pets!

Most large estates had their own animal cemeteries which were mostly for dogs. The Rhiwlas estate on the outskirts of Bala run by the larger than life character Richard Lloyd John Price supposedly had a hundred dogs at one time. Many are buried on a patch of land known as 'South America' after a former gardener compared it to a jungle! Several graves are dated during the 1880s and amongst them is a grave for "Comedy' the most loving of retrievers, shot accidently by her

Hafod y Porth burial ground

Poethlyn's grave

master 1887". Chirk Castle, Erddig, Nant -Eos near Aberystwyth and the Foelas estate in Pentrefoelas are also examples of large houses with a cemetery for their dogs.

Many farm dogs who end their days as grey muzzled, arthritic old timers with hoarse barks are given marked graves especially if there are children on the farm. I have seen several examples of gravestones made with roofing slates vividly painted by the child with the pet's name. These inevitably fade with time, weather and as the children grow older.

An island formed by the confluence of two streams was the traditional burying ground for dogs on the Hafod-y-Llan farm in Snowdonia, famously bought for the Snowdonia National Park following an appeal which was financially supported by Sir Anthony Hopkins in 1998. One, a popular collie bitch called 'Men' had to be put down by her owner after she was caught worrying sheep; a local poet wrote a touching 'englyn' for her in the 1950s.

I recently went in search of a horse's grave and the extraordinary story which came with it. It began in 1917 when a horse called 'Poethlyn' was discovered pulling a milk cart in the village of Overton near Wrexham and was taken off the streets to be trained as a racehorse. He was entered in the 1918 wartime version of the Grand National held in Gatwick, London and won! He was however denied the full kudos of his victory because it wasn't deemed the 'proper' Grand National. In 1919 following the cessation of hostilities the race was re-instated at Aintree and Poethlyn was entered again. Carrying a jockey who weighed twelve and a half stones, the heaviest in the history of the race. He won again to silence his critics! The jockey? Well, none other than Ernest Piggot; yes, Lester's grandfather!

Poethlyn was buried on Bryn y Pys estate in 1940 and I had to obtain special permission and a guide to see this difficult to find location which is very much overgrown and neglected. Poethlyn is in good company; lying next to him is 'Bryn Truthful', a greyhound which won the Waterloo cup twice! Also nearby is the grave of a Brown Bear which used to be a family pet.

Another horse whose grave is marked somewhat more auspiciously than Poethlyn's is 'Sir Briggs' whose ostentatious tomb is found in Tredegar Gardens, Newport. Sir Briggs carried Godfrey Morgan in the charge of the light brigade in 1854 one of the more famous military blunders in the Crimean War immortalized by Tennyson. Godfrey Morgan later became Lord Tredegar and 'Sir Briggs' lived another 20 years to be 28 years old. Seven hundred horses rode into that "valley of death" and only 195 rode back. A statue of Sir Briggs and Lord Tredegar stands in the centre of Cardiff.

In the snowy winter of 1925 high up in Cwm Brwynog, one of Snowdon's upland valleys a young mare called 'Bel' slipped in the snow on Christmas day and broke her leg. She was buried on the spot near the little cottage of Brithdir where a seven year old girl called Beryl lived. That Christmas, Beryl planted the holly sprig which had been used as their Christmas tree on Bel's grave. Seventy three years passed, then in 1998 as an old lady in her eighties and having lived in Devonport most of her life Beryl visited her old home and was delighted to find a healthy holly tree growing from 'Bel's last resting place!

Not so for poor old Lofty, a shire horse who died in harness on my uncle's farm in Anglesey when he was a young man in the 1930s. Lofty was buried at the side of the field where he dropped with nothing to mark his grave. Half a century later I happened upon a huge bone by the hedge one evening whilst I was out shooting rabbits; when I asked of its provenance I was told of poor old Lofty and how almost thirty years after his death Manweb decided to erect an electric pole right on the very spot where he was buried!

Two huge stones ten feet apart mark the grave of Lord Mostyn's horse 'Captain Morgan' on the bank of Llyn Helyg in Flintshire. Some say it was the horse that won the race on the old Babell racecourse which resulted in the jockey being gifted the Piccadilly Inn in appreciation, whether it's true or not, it's a good story!

In front of St. Mathew's church, Borth, Cardiganshire are the well tended graves of 'Lucky' 'Lucky II' and 'Chilli', I wonder what their stories are?

Not every animal memorial is necessarily a grave. The old Garth Inn some five miles west of Builth used by generations of drovers was once known as 'Hark to Statesman' in memory of 'Statesman' a famous otter hound. During Lord Coventry's Mastership of the Hawkstone otter hounds it seems that following one particular chase the hounds were called off the nearby river Irfon when the otter was lost. Statesman, however slipped back on his own and picked up the scent. In the 1980s the brewery were consulted and the old sign was re-painted.

There are several excellent examples of animals who have made their mark in some way or other who have earned themselves a memorial. Those walking the Anglesey coast path on the clifftops between Rhosneigr and Rhoscolyn will pass a relatively inconspicuous stone with writing on it, this is the memorial to 'Tyger' a Labrador who saved four sailors. It was a foggy September day in 1819 when a ketch bound for Liverpool hit an exposed reef called Maen Piscar half a mile offshore and almost immediately sank. Tyger could sense which way to swim through the fog and showed his master and three sailors the way ashore. He even returned to help the captain who was tiring rapidly. When they were safely ashore and had clambered up the rocks Tyger died of his exertions.

Swansea Jack too was a dog who earned his immortality by saving lives. He lived with his master William Thomas near the North dock in Swansea and during his seven years' life he jumped into the water several times whenever anyone got into difficulty. He reportedly saved 27 people and two dogs and was given a silver collar through public subscription in 1931. Five years later he was awarded the National 'Bravest Dog of the Year Award' sponsored by a London newspaper. Jack would appear at carnivals and other money raising events and in his short life received several bravery awards including the equivalent of a canine VC. He remains the only dog ever to receive two bronze medals by the National Canine Defence League. He died in 1937 after inadvertently eating rat poison. Jack's grave and memorial can be found on the promenade in Swansea.

By a strange coincidence another seaside dog named 'Jack' was also given a silver collar funded by public subscription in Llandrillo (Rhos on Sea) for his antics in a fish weir whose remains can still be seen at low tide. The 'Goret' was one of two on that shoreline and both could be traced back several centuries; however an 1861 act decreed that only the ones with evidence of ownership before the Magna Carta (1215) could be allowed to remain. Rhos Fynach weir was gifted to the monks of Maenan Abbey by Llywelyn Fawr in the 1198 Aberconwy

Charter; a document which still existed and was thus allowed to survive, a similar Goret a mile to the west was pulled down. It continued to be used up until the first world war when it fell into disrepair and was eventually removed by the sailing club.

It had been a very successful fish trap, in 1850 an estimated 35,000 mackeral were caught in a single tide! Another bumper night in 1907 saw ten tons of mackeral, many of these ended up as fertilizer on nearby fields. Jack was a little terrier trained by the Goret's owner John Evans to jump in and retrieve salmon and rapidly became a tourist attraction which explains the silver collar! Alas he was eventually bitten by a shark in 1873 and didn't survive his injuries. Sadly, as far as I know there is no known grave or memorial to Jack, but I thought he merited a mention.

Another seashore character from one of our cities was Billy the Seal who was caught in a fishing net in 1912 and made his

Talyllyn Railway Station Graves

home in a small zoo in Victoria park, Cardiff where he lived until 1939. Despite an attempted escape in 1927 when the river Ely burst its banks he remained a local favourite. Following a resurgence of interest in his story when the popular folk group 'The Hennessys' wrote a song for him a steel statue was erected in 1998. The irony was that Billy had turned out to be a female!

When Tal-y-llyn railway station in the Brecon Beacons closed in the early 1960s following widespread cuts there were three gravestones by the side of the platform. One was for 'Prince' the dog (1888) who lived for seven years, one for 'Dick' the blackbird (1887) who lived for fourteen years and a mock one for the railway staff who were awaiting Beeching's axe! Dick was the only one of three rescued chicks to survive when their parents died and was reared by the station staff. He was very tame and popular with the passengers. His story appears in 'Cymru'r Plant', a Welsh children's magazine in 1910. Both 'Prince' and 'Dick's gravestones were eventually moved to Brecon Museum.

What about 'Joe' the chough who was bought for ten shillings (50p) by a publican in Caernarfon from a Bethel quarryman who had rescued it from a nest about to be blasted? This was in 1960 and he was reared on liver, hard boiled eggs and chicken feed to become a tame bird who was frequently seen around the castle and the Caernarfon pubs for many years. Despite almost losing one eye he made a full recovery and established himself as one of the characters of Caernarfon throughout the early 60s; has he got a grave I wonder? Or 'Kelly' the goose who made the town of Conwy his home during the 1950s, I say he because Kelly turned out to be a gander. He escaped from a crate off a train in Llandudno Junction bound for a London poultry market and was adopted by a local garage owner. Kelly in turn adopted a patch of land near the castle from where he would see off any dog! He became a tourist favourite when he appeared on a postcard in 1952.

Sometime in the 1920s 'Bob' the raven of the Forest Arms, Brechfa shared the ignomy of immortality with Roy Rogers' horse 'Trigger' at the hands of a taxidermist; a not infrequent fate for cats I am told. 'Bob' had been tamed and trained by the landlord Joe Sivell and was famous for stealing caps and other objects. He also had a tendency to worry horses left tethered outside and had taken a particular dislike to the Vicar and would unearth plants and vegetables in the vicarage garden. When Joe's son Dudley retired he took Bob with him but I'm glad to say that he is now back in the Forest Arms where he can still be seen in his glass case.

Obviously I cannot write an account, however brief on animal burials without mentioning the most famous; Gelert. He was, as the story describes, Prince Llywelyn's faithful hound left behind to guard the baby while Llywelyn followed his priorities and went hunting! At some point a big bad wolf came and Gelert became embroiled in a violent fight to the death

Captain Morgan's Grave

118

with the wolf knocking the crib over in the struggle but managed to kill it and protect the baby. When Llywelyn returned he was greeted by Gelert with blood on his mouth, an overturned crib and no sign of the baby. In his anguish he drew his sword and killed Gelert only to find seconds later the body of the wolf and the unharmed baby. It is said Llywelyn never smiled again!

This is a very old story which can be traced back centuries to India where a pet mongoose protects a baby from a cobra. There is even an Arabic version involving a rat and a ferret! The poet Spenser wrote a ballad telling the story in 1800 whilst staying with Maddocks the builder of the sea wall in Porthmadog. The tale was then adopted by David Pritchard who built the Goat hotel in Beddgelert during the first decade of the century. It was he who constructed the grave as a tourist attraction which is visited by so many every year! Significantly when William Williams published his book 'Observations on

Black humour from Wepre

the Snowdon mountains' in 1802 in which he actually deals with such stories no mention is made of Gelert or his grave. Despite this lack of provenance to the story's credibility the flagstones around the grave remain moist with tears each summer.

Perhaps a less deliberate memorial was found beneath the walls of Carreg Cennen Castle, Llandeilo in the form of 43 leg tags dating from the 1920s. They all belonged to Racing Pigeons and are thought to have been victims of a Peregrine Falcon.

I have actually searched for some which I have heard about only to discover that they are no longer there. A good example of a disappointing search was for 'Queen' which was a donkey bought for the vicar of Llanrhaeadr, near Denbigh by the parishoners to carry him around the parish. When she died in 1910 she was buried in a field at the very centre of the vale and a stone with her name carved on it. Not only did I fail to locate it but couldn't find anyone local who had heard the story! Ah well!

The above examples merely scratch the surface of what I believe must be hundreds of interesting animal memorials and their stories within the Principality waiting to be told. If any reader feels they would like to share/contribute any stories towards a possible book I would be very grateful to receive them along with locations and/or photos which would be carefully copied, diligently returned and fully acknowledged in any such book.

Chapter 10

In the bowels of Moelwyn Mawr

The best learnt lessons are often the harsh ones which you survive. In this account of an abortive underground journey I have endeavoured to be as candid as possible about the mistakes I made and the tongue in cheek role a chap I met in a pub played in this adventure deep under a Welsh mountain.

The 'level walk in'

The entrance from Croesor

Twenty five Novembers ago I embarked on a trip into the very bowels of Moelwyn Mawr and as a result learnt two very valuable lessons. One was to check the accuracy of any adventure route description before venturing on it and the other to be wary of any information given by characters wearing paisley patterned cravats, sporting beards and smoking pipes! A tongue in cheek over-simplification perhaps but I would like to narrate what happened because I didn't double check one particular route description given by a character who happened to be dressed like that.

It had been one of those casual pub encounters and my bearded acquaintance had been telling me about the Croesor to Rhosydd through trip. "A level walk in, a slight climb followed by a simple abseil and an easy walk out". What could possibly go wrong?

And so, one Saturday morning two of us set off from Tanygrisiau, Blaenau Ffestiniog by the side of the playful little stream draining the lake above. We continued up through the beautiful valley of Cwmorthin past the lake which sports several slate spoil heaps which encroach fern like into its lower end. We

The exit into Rhosydd

Inside Rhosydd quarry

paused briefly by the melancholy little ruin of the old miner's chapel reflecting how everything changes with time. We continued up a steeper ramp to the upper cwm which holds Rhosydd quarry, its empty, roofless buildings stubbornly reminding us of its once glorious past. One cannot help wonder at the genius of Victorian engineering which harnessed every drop of rainwater to power the quarry.

Bearing left to reach the ridge that leads over to the old quarry of Croesor we passed the mouth of a tunnel which we assumed would be our egress some three hours later... Yeah well! We had intended being back for 'Final Score' and the equipment we carried represented both this intention and the level of difficulty we expected to find. I had a safety rope, a reasonable torch and a packed lunch. Gareth too had a packed lunch, a packet of polo mints and what looked suspiciously like a 'fischer price' torch.

We soon located the entrance to Croesor's underground quarry set high above the Croesor valley like an eyrie and our projected 'simple walk through the mountain'. We were looking forward to getting out of the cold wind, Gareth especially as he had stepped over his knees into a bog some fifteen minutes earlier.

The quarry had finally ceased operations in 1930 but the tunnel had been later adapted to store explosives for a nearby quarry until 1970. As a result the barred entrance looked like a jail door from an old cowboy film.

About 400 yards of level walking past a small waterfall issuing out of the ceiling of the tunnel seemed to confirm the veracity of our given description and we soon reached a wide chamber which was divided into three rooms. Pieces of old quarry equipment lay everywhere, fox coloured rails, locked in rust stood proud of the grey floor, and old bakelite electrical junction boxes adorned the walls. There was a still, dark lake whose clear waters revealed its frightening depth of cobalt blue in our torchlights. The characteristic smell of damp and dust pervaded everywhere and there, in front of us rising as described was the slight climb, it was just a steep ramp and our confidence was boosted by the simplicity of its ascent.

When we reached the ceiling and could climb no further we found ourselves on a sloping ledge with a ragged looking white rope snaking over a lip to our left into a black uninviting hole. In hindsight we had reached the final point where I could have avoided writing this story twenty five years on! Alas, fate does not share her fickle intentions with anyone so I began to unwind my rope and prepare for the "simple abseil".

Gareth went first whilst I provided a safety rope. The logic being, if the old rope broke I would save Gareth's life and he could buy me beer for ever. If the rope held it would presumably be safe for me to abseil without a safety rope. Half way down, with his torch in his mouth he shouted something and the torch fell and smashed to pieces. I hadn't heard what he said but I did catch the rich consonants in the words which followed.

My turn came, and without a safety rope my mouth was too dry to say anything. In one place, some twenty feet down the rock is so overhanging I found myself spinning like a spider; perhaps that had been what he had been trying to say. As I relaxed a new worry hit me, what if his dentures had fallen with the torch, would I have to look for them? A simple abseil it certainly was not!

We found ourselves in a massive chamber where you could fit a church or one of those double decker chapels found in

Site of the first abseil

quarry towns. My torch light was swallowed by the darkness long before it could reach anything to see. Any noise we made accentuated the echoey vastness of the cavern. The floor fell away in a chaotic rubble of sharp slates and giant boulders some of which had obviously fallen from the ceiling. Several of their pointed cousins seemed to be waiting Damocles-like for their own turn to fall. It was as if a demented giant had smashed up a cemetery. We heard one fall in the distance and the reverberating boom was very disconcerting. The whole place seemed to reinforce the sardonic irony of the "simple abseil" description and its emerging consequences as the very first shadow of doubt was cast on the wisdom of our adventure. It was time to look for the "easy walk out".

An hour later we were back at the foot of the abseil, sweaty, dishevelled and ever so slightly worried. Many of the slate piles were loose and movement over and through with only one torch was laborious. We had failed to find any hint of what was becoming the 'fabled way out' and amid the dawning realization that we were in over our heads without the necessary equipment to extricate ourselves I was beginning to form some very dark thoughts about my bearded ex-friend from the pub.

We ate our packed lunch in a muted air of developing misery and considered our next option. More in hope than expectation I made some prussik knots with my laces and cut a couple of slings from my rope to try and ascend the old rope but the knots either slipped or jammed and when one lace snapped I took it as a sign that we would not get out that way. I even tried to climb a smooth slab to the left of the abseil in the forlorn hope it would reach the sloping ledge but after twenty feet of holding the torch in my aching jaw I realized that too was not an option. At around this time we wryly noted that 'Final Score' had already started.

Leaving Gareth to probably curse ever meeting me I went for another sortie through what we later discovered has been daubed the 'chamber of horrors' to see if not having to share a torch might reveal the way out. It did, because far over to the left where the ceiling dips to almost ground level an opening the size of a front door awaited me, replete with another manky old abseil rope. It was like a giant letterbox; no wonder we'd missed it sharing a single torch. I returned for my companion. Then, as we negotiated our way back down Gareth slipped and sliced his wrist on a sharp flake of slate and we spent an anxious few minutes trying to stem the blood with a ripped off shirt pocket and length of lace which had, in a recent previous life been a prussic knot. Even in the dim light of our single torch his face was as grey as a dead tooth and the seriousness of our plight began to hit home.

The idea of another committing abseil further into the bowels of despair was not appealing but the hope that the "easy walk out" might well be at the foot of the abseil spurred us on. Once again we adopted the same rudimentary safety system and Gareth went first. It was another steep abseil but slightly shorter (which was a good thing as my rope was now at least two slings shorter). It held and I was duly robbed of a lifetime of free beer!

This time we were in a much smaller chamber and back at the water table level. We supposed it was only a short but underwater swim to the first chamber of several hours ago. So near but Oh so far. A pile of slate rubble was the only other feature, the easy walk out certainly didn't leap out to introduce itself. We then noticed a hole, no bigger than a manhole cover going down through the slate pile with a short knotted rope. We slid in like two suppositories and found ourselves ten feet lower on what was the true floor of the level, and lo and behold there were footprints! Halleluiah, the fabled "easy walk out"?

The banter returned in a wave of relieved euphoria as we followed the footprints through the sticky paste formed of slate dust and damp, I even began forgiving my bearded friend. And then, ever so abruptly the tunnel stopped on the lip of a water pit with steep sides and an old decrepit bridge crossing unappealingly to where the tunnel could be seen continuing beyond. It was a single beam of wet, rotten timber as wide as a railway sleeper devoid of any handrails and neither of us fancied balancing across; we were sure there would be other options to by-pass it.

There weren't, and half an hour later I was mentally preparing to cross the bridge. The water below was still, dark and deep, the wood was so soft you could dig your finger in and although I had the rope bowlined to my waist I knew if the bridge failed or I fell in there would be very little realistic chance of my getting out. My heart was thumping as I gingerly balanced across.

Beyond, the tunnel continued for another thirty yards until I reached yet another smooth walled pit with water ten feet below. This time the bridge had collapsed and the only way across would have been to climb across the steep wall to the right. I could see the route and its feasibility but without safety gear and a companion to belay the rope I decided it was too dangerous. Better to have to snuggle Gareth to keep warm than tread water for the rest of my hypothermic life.

And it was then, at that moment that realization finally hit me, this was indeed the way out but not for us, today. We had

The bridge

embarked on a trip far more advanced than two friends out for a day's jolly had prepared for. Without the neccessary gear we were well and truly trapped underground.

Another tense crossing of the bridge and we were re-united for another discussion of options. There were two; either make a nest by the bridge or make a nest somewhere nearer the ten foot hole. And thus, using a map, rope and two rucsacs as groundsheets we made a nest as comfortless as a cormorant's and settled on a small rise above the grey sludge which contained those teasing footprints, to await rescue.

We both had a shirt, fleece and a waterproof and despite knowing the temperature at this depth would remain a constant 10 degrees celsius I also knew the wet atmosphere would make us very cold very quickly. As well as the torch I also had a six inch candle stump and a 'club orange' chocolate bar; Gareth had half a packet of polo mints.

Any residual banter evaporated like morning mist inside two minutes of switching off the light as we both descended into our private thoughts. We had done some energetic activity over the last few hours and shared some intensive thoughts and fears; it seemed a period of silent contemplation was now needed.

After an hour of sweat cooling misery I declared I would go and have another 'look around' just in case we had missed an obvious escape route through a small side tunnel hidden in the shadows or something equally unlikely, besides we needed a warm up.

It was the inevitable dejavu; all tunnels led back to that accursed bridge and I found myself teetering across one more time for a final confirmation that the next pit could not be crossed without a very necky solo climb. We returned to our 'nest'.

Our spirits rose and fell like a yo yo and through it all the cold damp penetrated deeper into our bones. We both knew the temperature would only cause discomfort and would not be a threat to survival, we also knew there was plenty of water to drink; I idly wondered which part of Gareth I would eat first.

For three minutes every hour we lit the candle and did some exercises, and just confirmed our existence. Sometimes we cheated and lit it early or kept it going an extra two minutes. That candle was our umbilical with reality and the fingers on our watches gave us the only perception of passing time. Occasionally a piece of ceiling fell and the disconcerting echoe boomed down the tunnel to set our hearts racing. There were moments of humour. I shared my concern that a chilli I had in the slo-cooker would go furry; his worry was that the supply teacher who would inevitably be called in to cover his absence would discover three months of marking which hadn't been done in his class's Welsh books! I had to laugh.

We had analysed, interpreted and calculated our chances of being rescued and how long before that happened. There were several 'what ifs?' the most worrying of which was what if Gareth had forgotten to lock the car as he often did? If it was stolen nobody would know where to look for us. Despite the projected simplicity of the trip we had committed the cardinal sin of not telling anyone where we were going!

The passing hours merged into a numbing slowness which defied our best guesses at how long had passed. Three or four 'cuddling to keep warm' positions had evolved to host short cat naps in between shivering and the welcome exercise for those precious three minutes every hour. It was as if the very concept of time had become distorted with nothing to give it substance.

A couple of times we had heard some unexplained noises which we put down to moving slates or our imagination. Were the fabled 'knockers' the old miners believed existed real? A strange sense of accepting our plight had peacefully descended on us.

And then, suddenly we heard a muffled shout! "Hello, is there anybody there?" like a parody from a classic victorian séance. We both answered together. The voice had carried from the top of the first abseil and it would be another twenty minutes before two of the rescue team lads emerged. We were told to stay put. We shared the club orange (I still have the wrapper as a book mark in the section of a book describing the quarry). It was difficult to convey how grateful we felt as we shook hands and thanked them for coming. A strong feeling of humility mixed with embarrassment was also a dominant feature of our thoughts.

Despite being cold and stiff, after some hot tea from a thermos we were soon climbing through the ten foot hole and getting ready to climb the rope using SRT clamps. Ascending the lower abseil soon warmed us up. The huge chamber of shattered slates above was lit like a discotheque as we made our way to the foot of the top abseil.

Less than an hour later we were walking out along the Croesor level past the little waterfall and out into fresh air. Although the mist was right down where the tunnel emerges at over 1600 feet above sea level in the upper Croesor valley and it was raining it was wonderful to be walking back down the mountain to the car. And yes, Gareth had left it unlocked!

Our gratitude to the lads of the Aberglaslyn Mountain Rescue team is absolute but thanks too to Jan for noticing my absence and to Dafydd and Pete for working out where we'd gone. They had wisely declined the offer to accompany us!

I returned a month later with some friends and proper equipment which included a small inflatable boat to cross one of the lakes to complete the trip (Gareth decided not to come). It was certainly an adventure but that is quite another story.

Today, the trip is still done by experienced groups with many of the sections now permanently laced with extra wires, ropes and aluminium ladders as safeguards. It is still an adventure and it can still be dangerous.

By now I have long forgiven the pipe smoking bearded character wearing a paisley cravat whose grossly inaccurate route description persuaded two friends to venture on a day's jolly deep into the bowels of Moelwyn Mawr. Perhaps the bridges were all in place when he did it, or the water not as high, or indeed, perhaps he only really did the trip in his imagination.

Chapter 11

Race to Ireland

Most people are aware of the brave exploits and 'firsts' by famous aviators like Amy Johnson, Amelia Earhart, Charles Linderburgh and Antoine de Saint Exupery whose early pioneering flights paved the way for the global travel of today. Here is a short account of the early attempts to fly across the Irish Sea 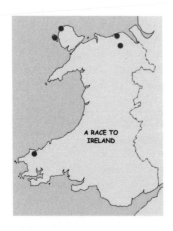 using Wales as their starting point. The death of one, the almost farcical near misses, and the mishaps they all endured shows just how close to the limit of what was possible they all had to reach in these audacious attempts.

Home made glider near Bodfari
© *Modest Millionaire (W.Hywel) Gwasg Gee 1973*

On the 17th December 1903 arguably one of mankind's most significant technological leaps forward occurred when Orville and Wilbur Wright succeeded in the world's first powered flight in something heavier than air. And although it only lasted twelve seconds and covered a mere 120 feet it ranks with harnessing fire, inventing the wheel and splitting the atom. Although Bill Frost of Pembrokeshire had succeeded In flying his creation for 500 yards in 1895 it was a cross between a gas balloon and a crude helicopter and not an aeroplane in the now accepted definition.

Despite the Wright brothers' reluctance to go public for another three years due to patenting concerns they couldn't hold back this tide of interest which was becoming global. It heralded a new era which saw a frenzy of well heeled but daring young men and women experimenting, competing and pushing the boundaries of 'aeroplaning' as it was then known. Driven by a sense of adventure, ego and prize money for set races, distances covered, and seas crossed those 'magnificent men in their flying machines' had caught the public imagination and were regularly making the headlines across the world.

The first flight in Britain was made by Samuel Cody at Farnborough in 1908 and in 1909 the first flight across the English Channel was achieved by Louis Bleriot winning the considerable prize of a thousand pounds. Using this money he began manufacturing his own planes and set up two flying schools in France to sell them!

These early planes were made of canvass and wood supported by little more than bicycle wheels and underpowered by engines rarely pushing more than 25 horse power. The pilots weren't even strapped in; in 1912 Harriet Quimby was killed when turbulence threw her out of her plane a few weeks after she became the first woman to fly the Channel! In 1910 there were 33 fatalities, 65 in 1911 and in 1912 as many as 95 aeroplaners were killed in pursuit of their passion.

In 1910 a flamboyant London based actor called Robert Loraine unwittingly began a race which reached a climax in April

1912 which involved a man who had been brought up in Bodfari. North Wales. It was a race to be the first to fly across the Irish Sea and it has a script straight out of a Holywood adventure film!

Loraine set off from Blackpool on August 10th flying a bi-plane built and designed by Henry Farman, a Briton living in France. Less than a month earlier he had been the first to land on the Isle of Wight. His navigational plan was to follow the coast to Holyhead but due to some sea mist was forced to land on Rhos on Sea golf course. The Greenkeeper apparently came out in his pyjamas

Robert Loraine
© *Wiki commons*

to register his indignation! He then continued to Holyhead but ran out of petrol and had to land in a field near Llanfair-yng-Nghornwy on the NW tip of Anglesey. He set off once again for Holyhead on August 12th but crashed on take off slightly damaging the undercarriage, he himself was uninjured. By now people were flocking to see the spectacle on Mynachdy farm and the enterprising farmer was charging threepence for a glass of water and a shilling for a glass of milk! He later billed Loraine for fifty six pounds because the visiting crowds had damaged his fields! September 4th he made another attempt but crashed again slightly injuring himself. By September 11th he'd had the plane removed to what is now Penrhos nature reserve in Holyhead and once again he set off, this time successfully. No doubt taking a proverbial deep breath he turned west and aimed his fragile plane for Ireland. Comical as some of these antics were this was a serious undertaking and Loraine had guts. Five times whilst over the sea his engine almost cut out due to a problem with the fuel pipe but recovered each time just before his flimsy craft hit the waves. Eventually he sighted land and he must have felt he was going to make it, but then disaster struck. Suddenly two of his controlling wires snapped and he was unable to keep the plane in the air; he went down into the sea a mere 400 yards from shore! He had reached the Baily lighthouse and was so close to success. In keeping with the almost farcical series of mishaps he swam the final few hundred yards and despite claiming to have been the first to fly across the Irish Sea his claim wasn't accepted by the 'aeroplaning fraternity'.

Ironically he was appearing in a play in London within two days called 'The man from the sea!'

Loraine became a decorated and wounded hero of the Great War and was involved in several aerial 'dogfights'. Credited with coining the term 'joystick' he retired with the rank of Major. He went on to make a successful acting career and lived until 1935.

Surprisingly it was to be another eighteen months before the 'race to Ireland' was continued, and this time there were three contenders.

Damer Leslie Allen and Denys Corbett Wilson were friends

Leslie Allen
© *Wiki commons*

who both flew from Hendon aerodrome north of London. They both had their eyes on the Irish prize and they decided to make the attempt together. The plan to follow the railway line to Holyhead shows how rudimentary aerial navigation was in those early days. It was April 17th when Wilson set off followed twelve minutes later by Allen. A mechanic was scheduled to meet both aviators in Chester. Allen landed somewhere in Cheshire to get his bearings and flew on

Denys Corbett Wilson © Wiki commons

almost immediately to land on the racecourse in Chester where he was met by the mayor and his retinue of welcome. Meanwhile Wilson had lost his compass overboard in the buffeting winds and had landed on a farm near Hereford where his initial reception was decidedly frosty.

The 85 mile leg to Holyhead took Allen only two hours and his plane was seen passing over the town at 8.15 heading west. Allen was considered a novice and was carrying neither a cork life vest or, as was the fashion an inflated inner tube. To all intent and purpose it seemed a reckless venture; but in all honesty weren't they all, if measured by today's standards? Tragically, Leslie Allen was never seen again except for one of the plane's wheels which was washed ashore some time later.

Meanwhile, correctly guessing that Allen was ahead Wilson had decided to re-fuel at Hereford and continue without the advice and support of his mechanic. Unfortunately he put in the wrong type of lubricant which resulted in the engine mis-firing forcing him to put down on a hilly field near Colva, Radnorshire. His luck was in and he managed to land with only yards to spare

The plaque in the field near Goodwick

before hitting a wall. He was to be there a further three days waiting for his mechanic to arrive. By then it was likely that Allen's fate was known to him and he decided to alter his plans and attempt the shorter leg from Fishguard across St. George's Channel; a decision which would later come back to nag him.

Once the correct grade of castor oil had been put in the engine he set off again and landed in Goodwick near Fishguard on April 21st where his mechanic joined him for a thorough service of the plane. He had taken five days to come from Hendon.

Then, finally on the morning of the 22nd at 6.0am he set off in perfect weather for the south of Ireland. When he was 15 miles out he hit a squall which he couldn't climb out of. His engine started to splutter and he had great difficulty maintaining course in the now blustery wind. It was a worrying period which improved considerably when he spotted fields below in a break in the clouds. Just two miles short of Enniscorthy he crash-landed with a failing engine and ended up on a stone faced bank; although the plane was damaged he was unhurt. Denys Corbett Wilson was the first to fly from Wales to Ireland. It had taken an hour and forty minutes.

Lavish feting was to follow this success by the people of

Wexford and much was made of the fact he was an Irishman!

Wilson went on to join the Royal Flying Corps which was formed around the time of his success and although he briefly gave up flying in 1913, he re-joined the RFC when war broke out.

In the early stage of the war friendly fire was as much a danger as the German guns due to the ground observers mistaking the underwing emblems of both nations especially when looking into the sun. The now familiar circle target was introduced to stop this happening. Unfortunately Wilson and his navigator were shot down and killed by 'friendly' fire in 1915.

Returning to those feverish few days in April 1912 another man who had been planning and coveting being first to fly the Irish Sea had been caught hopping when news reached him of these attempts. He raced back from London to his base in Rhyl to put his plane together; his name was Vivian Hewitt.

Hewitt was from a wealthy Brewery family from Grimsby but had been brought up in Warren House, Bodfari. He had always been interested in engines and had constructed his own 14 inch gauge railway in the grounds of the house on the Mold-Denbigh road. When he took up an interest in flying he built his own glider which he had flown off Pant Glas hill above the valley. In 1909 he moved to and rented a shed at Brooklands where, as well as racing cars (he was the test driver for Singer) he had his own aeroplane. By 1911 he was back in Rhyl where he rented rooms near the Foryd and had a small private aerodrome on

Vivian Hewitt-
© *Wikipedia Historic wings magazine*

Warren House, Bodfari

Gratton farm which used to be near the Marine Lake. Like many of these early pioneers he would conduct displays in a similar way to the American barn stormers. He, like Wilson and Allen had a Bleriot XI monoplane with a 50 horse power Gnome engine which he had bought in 1910 for eleven hundred pounds, money provided by his uncle.

Hewitt set off from Rhyl on the 22rd of April still unaware at that stage that Wilson had succeeded, knowing only an 'aeroplaner had been lost at sea'. He was aiming for Holyhead and the trip should have taken less than an hour. Unfortunately he encountered strong winds which blew him out over the sea and he had quite a tricky time with the engine fully opened to get back over the land. He landed in a field on Plas Llanfrydog farm near Llanerchymedd in wind which at times blew him backwards. The following day he made it to Holyhead but had three anxious days of waiting until the weather improved.

Finally, at 10.30 am on April 26th and cheered by a large crowd Vivian Hewitt took off for Ireland. There was little more than a haze when he set off but half way across he encountered a thick bank of fog with visibility only as far as his wingtips. He carried no compass and when he emerged from the fog he used the sun as a rough directional guide.

There would have been times on that flight when he thought of Leslie Allen and what may have gone wrong for him, and like others before him on such committing flights over open sea he would have known that any mishap which resulted in the plane going down would have meant death, despite the inflated inner tube draped around his shoulder. He must have been very relieved when he sighted land. He then realized that he was flying over the Wicklow mountains, and had been blown over forty miles off course!

Eventually he located Dublin and followed the Liffey over the city to execute a perfect landing in Phoenix Park. He had done what he had set out to do. All day he had crowds and journalists eager to see both him and his machine as he was entertained by a succession of arriving dignitaries. Although both Wilson and Hewitt's stories made the papers the recent news of Scott and his men's demise in the Antarctic was still raw as was the April 15th sinking of the Titanic; two tragedies that would inevitably have detracted from the newsworthiness of the airmen's successes .

The plane was crated up and shipped back to Holyhead and thus began the niggling but civilly conducted question "Who really was the first to cross the Irish Sea?" Was it Loraine in 1910 when he had to swim the last few hundred yards? Was it Wilson who had opted for the shorter St. George's Channel or was it Vivian Hewitt who, four days later had crossed what had become to be the expected route?

He returned to Rhyl where a tremendous welcome awaited him much as Wilson had enjoyed by his Irish countrymen. He was proclaimed as the first man to cross the Irish Sea from Holyhead to Dublin; a careful choice of words!

When war broke out Hewitt applied to join the RFC but

wasn't pronounced fit enough. Instead he went to America where he became the test pilot for the Curtis Aircraft company. A crash near the end of the war left him with injuries which prevented him flying again. In 1919 he went to live in the Bahamas. When his uncle died in 1930 he inherited a vast fortune and returned to live on Anglesey where he began the most eccentric period of his life. He bought a solitary house right next to the sea near Cemlyn Bay. The house was called Bryn Aber and he immediately employed eight men (one of whom was my uncle Wil) to build a huge wall around the grounds. He also developed a bird sanctuary nearby which is still managed by the National Trust. He began collecting artefacts that only a multi millionaire could collect. Valuable stamps, powerful racing cars, yachts, thousands of bird's eggs, tools (some of which he never used), and stuffed animals. He had two Great Auks which had been extinct since

Bryn Aber, Anglesey

1834 and were at the time worth six thousand pounds each. One room was kept for eight pet parrots.

Hewitt never married but was friendly with his housekeeper from Rhyl who moved to Bryn Aber with her son to look after him. It is far beyond the scope of this chapter to delve any deeper into his quirky lifestyle; how he would take delivery every two months of five thousand pounds in five pound notes and insist their numbers were in sequence for example or pretend he was the gardener whenever he had an unexpected visitor! How he would only drink rainwater collected from a tank on the roof and how he refused to have electricity despite having bought a generator which he never used!

Eventually he moved back to Nassau in the Bahamas to avoid paying income tax (and this from a man who had lent the Exchequer fifty thousand pounds for the war chest in 1940).

Vivian Hewitt died in 1965 and despite the intensely colourful and eccentric life he led before and after 1912 he will always be remembered as the man who may have been first to fly across the Irish Sea.

When next you fly or ferry across to the Emerald Isle spare a thought for those four brave young men who sat in their flimsy wood and canvas crates and dared to fly across sixty miles of open sea wearing only an inflated car inner tube or a cork life vest as the woefully inadequate but only concession to safety!

Chapter 12

The Hyddgen Triangle?

Many readers will be familiar with the coined phrase 'Bermuda Triangle' which refers to an area of sea east of Florida and north of the Bahamas where several ships and planes have come to grief over the years. Perhaps some will have read the 'Welsh Triangle', a book written in 1979 by Peter Paget describing  several UFO sightings in a small area of the Pembrokeshire coast. I have 'borrowed' the phrase 'triangle' for this chapter.

Gelligogau

In 1865 the Rev. Donald Carr wrote a short book recounting his experience of surviving overnight in a snow storm on the Long Mynd in Shropshire. He had pastoral care for the parish of Ratlinghope as well as his own in Wolstaston; both either side of the mountain, and it was his custom to conduct a late afternoon service in Ratlinghope before returning home. The distance between the two churches is only four miles and he had done the trip many times.

Having encountered deep snow on the way there he had sent his servant back with the horses. It was whilst attempting to return home in worsening conditions and having unwisely declined the offer of accommodation that his ordeal began. It makes harrowing reading. Late the following day he was found wandering deliriously in the Carding Mill Valley by some children and subsequently rescued; he lived another 35 years.

In these days of cars and street lights this shouldn't happen. Even mountain walkers who deliberately place themselves in such potential danger have access to weather forecasts, phones and quality equipment; becoming lost in a snow storm is a rare event today. But in the past things were different. Anyone crossing the Migneint moors south of the A5 cannot fail to be impressed by their remoteness, even with the narrow umbilical strip of tarmac cutting through its vastness. On the top you may have noticed a cottage on the right just before the first bridge which crosses the infant Conwy. This is Llyn Cottage and was once part of the Penrhyn estate. At the beginning of last century Anna Jane from Penmachno was the housekeeper here and would walk the long track up from the village to her place of work. One winter's afternoon as she set off on her journey from the valley some light feathers of snow were just beginning to fall. By the time she reached the plateau however the snow was much heavier and had started to drift. Her employer at the cottage hadn't been expecting her due to the weather and because of this a search was not organized when she didn't arrive. Her family down in the valley where the snow was lighter had no reason for concern. She was found the next day frozen to death less than a hundred yards from the cottage.

The imposing mountain rising out of the moors to the south east is Arenig Fach, and on its summit there is a special cairn called 'Carnedd y Bachgen' which translates as the 'Boy's Cairn'. It was here that Dafydd, a nine year old shepherd from Weirglodd Ddu was found having been lost over night in heavy fog; he had frozen to death; and the poor little mite was found with his bare feet wrapped in his cap. It brings to mind young John Closs who tried to follow his mother and became lost on the snowy slopes of Moel Eilio in 1805; he too succumbed to the cold before he was found.

Twelve miles south as the crow flies a member of St. Athan Mountain rescue team, Michael Aspen has a memorial on Drws Bach ridge which connects Aran Fawddwy with y Drysgol; he was struck by lightning and killed in 1960 whilst out on exercise with the team.

A melancholy obelisk carved with an englyn by Eben Fardd is a memorial to David Davies, the young heir of Hendre Fechan

Obelisk for David Davies, Hendre Fychan

Sian Groca's stone

lies hidden in scrubland just south of Beddgelert after he too was killed by lightning in 1853. His sister who was standing beside him was unscathed.

And as my research increased so too did the long litany of such incidents, many of them sad 'if only' type stories, some were as a result of foolhardy decisions, and others, were just unlucky. But the more of these historical incidents I found, the more intrigued I became with one particular area in a remote tract of the Cambrian mountains of Mid Wales.

It seems that no less than seven people had perished in adverse weather conditions in one small area; all within a triangle whose longest side is only nine miles long!

One of the earliest recorded incidents involved a travelling pedlar called Sian Groca. She frequently traded in the area between Machynlleth and Llanidloes and would walk a path which roughly followed the river Severn. A section of this route traverses over the 2000 foot contour and it was just below this exposed col between Pumlumon and its neighbour Pumlumon Arwystli that she too was found dead one winter. The spot is marked by a rock strangely resembling a figure leaning forward as if carrying a heavy backback.

Tucked snugly into a little mountain valley less than half a minute's flight north by one of the mountain's ravens from where Sian Groca died is the ruined cottage of Gelligogau. In 1703, Catrin, the young wife of Rolant Wmffre of Gelligogau was on her way home from Machynlleth when she was caught in a fierce thunderstorm. She had been travelling in company with her neighbour from Bugeilyn, a homestead higher up the valley which was on her route. The two women took leave of each other at Bugeilyn and she continued alone for her final two miles down the valley. When night came and she hadn't arrived Rolant and a miner who was lodging with them in Gelligogau went out and searched until the early hours, but to no avail. Sometime in the morning her dog came home and led them to a large area of marsh known as the Llechwedd Crin. Here they

Bugeilyn

found her cloak and her basket. She had become disorientated in the storm and probably walked into a quagmire; she was expecting their first baby. Known as Cati Wen, her ghost is said to haunt the lonely valley on stormy nights and no shepherd would ever go near the ruins of the cottage after dark.

Pumlumon has never been a popular mountain in the way that the peaks of Snowdonia or Cadair Idris have been. Many of the early travel writers dismissed it as a "sodden weariness" including Thomas Pennant who shunned it completely. As the first mountain range to greet the prevailing south westerly weather systems it is perhaps no accident that the longest river in the UK as well as the prettiest are both born here. The sources of the Severn and the Wye are only two miles apart whilst the third of Pumlumon's daughters, the Rheidiol starts her short tempestuous journey to Aberystwyth as Nant y Llyn draining Llyn Llygad Rheidol, the lake just below the mountain's northern brow. Despite the attempts of two reservoirs to tame her this lively river doesn't begin to calm until she's finished her dramatic plunge through the gorge she created below Devil's Bridge.

The main Hengwm valley which drains this side of Pumlumon is about as wet and remote as anywhere in Wales. It has several side valleys each contributing a sizeable stream and at its head some five miles above Nant y Moch reservoir there is a large boggy depression which is one of the most significant watersheds in Wales. This is Cors Ebolion and rain falling here will either flow down the Llwyd and the Clywedog into the Severn and out into the Bristol Channel or if falling a few yards to the west becomes the Hengwm and joins the Rheidiol to enter the Irish sea. It is a desolate, lonely area and in snow and mist a very dangerous one.

It was near this unforgiving wet bowl at the head of the infant Clywedog in 1879 that Tom Lloyd became lost in heavy snow. He was a shepherd at Llwyn-y-gog farm near Staylittle and was on his way home late one evening after spending some time in the Star Inn, Dylife. Tom wasn't found for three days, but he was alive; barely. They took him down to Dyfngwm Isaf farm where they tried to warm him in front of a peat fire. Unfortunately the sudden change in temperature killed him, he is buried in Llawryglyn cemetery. His niece, whom I remember as an old lady of ninety was actually born during the three days he was out on the hillside.

A version of this story appears in 'Straeon y Pentan' written by Daniel Owen, Wales' first successful novelist. In the story which is published in 1895 his name is disguised as William and in Owen's novel he witnesses a corpse candle funeral a few days before his death, a sure portent of his own demise.

Barely a mile away is Llyn Bugeilyn which interestingly is known for its peculiar hunched back trout. The trout were supposedly stocked from Gelligogau stream by a retired sea captain from Machynlleth early in the nineteenth century.

Dyfngwm Isaf

149

Above the lake a ruined farmhouse, one of many in the area bears testimony to the depopulation which has ravaged the community of this rural upland this past century.

Here Ifan Crowdder once lived and farmed with his family. The Crowdders lived at Bugeilyn for eight generations. It was five o'clock on a snowy January 1763 when Ifan set off home from Esgair Fochnant farm near the village of Aberhosan. His route home although only three miles involved climbing almost a thousand feet following a small stream through a deep ravine to reach the plateau and the track to his home. The gorge is substantial and the terrifying drop to one side meant he had to be very careful. The snow however was so deep the upper reaches of the stream were buried and he somehow found himself lost on the unforgiving hinterland of Llechwedd Crin to the west of the house. Ifan's body wasn't found for three weeks. How ironic that Ifan's mother had been the last person to see Catrin Gelligogau alive as they walked home together from Machynlleth sixty years previously!

When I ventured to find the next venue of this sad list I decided to use my mountain bike, cycle the two miles to Bugeilyn along the track Ifan Crowedder so desperately wanted to find and descend the Hengwm valley. My daughter Megs came with me as, like myself, she too loves this wild corner of Pumumon.

The track from Bugeilyn continued for another mile seducing us with its ease, we could even manage a conversation appreciating the wild unspoilt setting as we cycled. But then, the track abruptly ends where a landrover could just about turn around and we were literally plunged into a world of tussock grass, rushes, sphagnum moss and black peat.

On our left where the infant stream was thinking about forming, a huge area of peat hags topped with scrawny heather rose out of the bog like purple and black mushrooms. Beyond, the slope began to rise towards the source of the Severn, broad ridges which would become Pumlumon and some of her wet sisters. The distant white boulders known as Y Fuwch Wen a'i Llo (The White Cow and her Calf) could be seen on the steepening slopes rising towards the source of the Severn.

As we struggled gamely down the valley every so often a wetter than usual section needed crossing as one of the many streams percolated itself through the marsh to join the rapidly growing Hengwm. By the time we crossed the third stream all attempts to keep our feet dry had ended. One small ravine even entailed a short carry. In the distance we could see the ruined cottage of Gelligogau nestling in its sheltered niche up the little valley and thought of poor Cati... and stormy nights!

Eventually the abandoned ruins of Lluest Newydd and Hengwmmannedd appeared like stubborn molars protruding out of the rushes. One gable end of Hengwmmannedd is still sporting a drainpipe. An old bedstead and a water tank rusted down to its skeletal frame are the only other signs it had ever been a home. The valley rising behind promised a future day of walking

'Y Fuwch Wen a'i llo'

as enticing little waterfalls and attractive cataracts beckoned, we both promised ourselves to come back. An amusing little outcrop of rock known as 'Ty'r Offeiriad' (the 'Priest's House') stood guard to the valley entrance whilst higher up 'Craig yr Eglwys' ('Church Rock') with its pointed 'spire' punctured the skyline.

More hard pedalling through squeaky rushes and squelching peat and we were rewarded with a footbridge to cross the Hengwm and reach a stony track. This however was a tease because very soon we had to re-cross the orangey-black water using a ford; and wet muddy feet become wet clean feet as we reached the track that would lead us up the Hyddgen valley.

We were now in Owain Glyndwr country where the nation's favourite hero enjoyed his greatest victory in 1401. Outnumbered three to one and surrounded by Flemish mercenaries he did the unexpected and charged to scatter his enemies leaving 200 of them dead. Two white boulders called the 'Covenant Stones' traditionally commemorate the battle

The lonely upland valleys of Hengwm and Hyddgen.

David Richards' plaque

and stand just the other side of the brackish black Hyddgen stream meandering sluggishly to join the Hengwm for the final half mile before being swallowed by the Nant y Moch reservoir.

Soon the ruins of Hyddgen farmhouse could be seen, now only a flattened mound of rubble and broken slate hidden in nettles, nearby a modern sheep shed already orange with rust dominates the site.

David Richards and his wife Jane lived here with their eight children. It was March 28th 1901 and David had gone to Beudy'r Hafod, a farm just over the ridge to the north and lower down the valley to pick up supplies which had been delivered there. On his way home he had been caught in a snow storm. When darkness fell Jane went to look for him and found him half dead less than a mile from the house. Despite being a small framed woman she managed to half drag and half carry him on her shoulders back to the house. He lived another 48 hours before dying. Before the following winter Jane moved her family down to Forge where she was the school caretaker for many years, she lived until 1940. A small cairn of white stones stood for decades marking the spot where David Richards was found but was disturbed when the Forestry Commission opened operations in the area. A brass plaque on a large quartz boulder has now replaced the cairn.

Our route took us past the small tarnished plaque. It is sad and evocative and tells of another age before land rovers and mountain bikes came to shorten the distances and devalue the remoteness offered by these hills. We continued to join another track eventually returning to Bugeilyn past cairns and hollows which eloquently speak of Glyndwr's sojourn in this romantic corner of the Cambrian mountains; a story which is excellently told in several books.

Three miles away to the south west as our raven flies is another slope near a conifer plantation. It is steep and dotted with feral pines some ten minutes' scramble above the Nant y Moch reservoir. It was here on this lonely mountain side that Lewis Mazon died in 1815. He too was on his way home from Machynlleth in snow and somehow fell off his pony. The pony made its way home to Geufaes and when they found Lewis in the morning both he and his corgi dog 'Cwic' had both died from the cold. Having travelled over eighteen miles they were just two miles from the safety of Geufaes. The incident has been immortalised in the ballad by the poet Grugog, 'Hen Nadolig Cymru' (The old Welsh Christmas).

The seventh fatal incident as a direct result of inclement weather in this area happened half a mile north of the reservoir and within sight of the victim's home, Dolrhuddlan. It was February 1845 and Morgan Morgan decided to accompany his daughter who was working in Lluesgota a couple of miles away because a recent period of heavy rain had swollen the stream she would have to cross. It was whilst he was leading the horse across afon Camddwr with his daughter riding that the current proved too strong. They were all washed away; fortunately his daughter and the horse made it to the side. Morgan wasn't so fortunate. His body was found the following day just a mile short of Aberystwyth. He had been taken in the flood and carried

Dolrhuddlan

through Rheidiol's angry gorges, his clothes had been torn from his body and he had suffered severe mutilations on the numerous rocks he had been dragged through.

Others have wandered lost on these barren slopes, many others in fact, walkers and travellers; some have died. But there is a heightened sense of injustice somehow when people perish within reach of their own homes. There is also perhaps a sense of irony when shepherds, drovers and pedlars come to grief treading paths they have walked so often and know so well.

The Reverand Donald Carr had made the four mile crossing over the Long Mynd over two thousand times when he almost came to grief that January night in 1865. Analysis of the incident shows that the easterly wind he had been battling had taken a subtle shift to the south and in continuing to push against it he had unwittingly gone in the wrong direction and had slid down a steepening slope into a ravine. He emerged out of this ravine late the following day to tell his tale.

Paradoxically, for a small hill the second largest death toll by avalanche in Britain occurred on the Long Mynd in 1772 when seven people were killed; the Reverend Carr should have remembered that.

It is perhaps fanciful to daub this relatively small area around Nant y Moch the 'Hyddgen Triangle'. But one cannot escape the irrefutable fact that all seven of these people knew their patch, their land and the weather it was capable of producing, but were still caught out and paid the ultimate price. Their sad tales remain an indictment on how any terrain and severe weather can combine to overwhelm the most experienced country person even in their own 'back yard'.

Safety in familiar surroundings are not a 'given' especially it would seem in the 'Hyddgen Triangle'.

Geufaes

Chapter 13

Violet's Leap

She was a criminal, attractive and sophisticated, but still a criminal. Why, therefore I ask myself have I injected something other than condemnation into this story of a woman who, once this tale was done vanished into the mists of time?

Violet Charlesworth

The North Wales Cycle path hugging the coast west of Conwy utilizes in part the old pre 1932 road and having cycled it several times can recommend it as good value for money. At Penmaen-bach Head where the first of the A55 tunnels appears when heading east the old road dramatically contours around on the very edge of the cliffs which plunge down to the sea when the tide is in. Stormy weather from the north carrying a high tide will often hurl the tops of breaking waves and sand over the old road.

On the very apex of the bend there is a prominent buttress of rock which is fun to clamber up called the 'Devil's Thumb'; it is also known as the 'Giant's Thumb'. A hundred yards further towards Conwy is a spot known as 'Violet's Leap' which made national headlines for a few days in 1909... and this is the story of Violet's Leap.

"Did she fall or was she pushed" was a phrase coined by the newspapers reporting a seemingly tragic incident on the cliffs of Penmaen-bach on the 4th January 1909. It was the early hours of the morning when a man named Roberts heard the noise of a

Spot from where she jumped

car engine (a rarity in those days) followed by breaking glass. When he went to investigate he found a top of the range Belgium Minerva car with a broken windscreen lodged on the wall overhanging the cliffs threatening to topple into the sea. A young lady named Eileen Charlesworth was very distressed claiming her sister Violet had fallen over the edge and disappeared. The chauffeur stood nearby seemingly in a state of shock.

Despite several searches immediately after the incident and over the next couple of days all that was found was her Tam o'Shanter hat and her diary.

Devil's Thumb

Violet Charlesworth was an attractive, articulate twenty four year old heiress who stood to inherit a hundred thousand pounds on her twenty fifth birthday which was only a few days away.

Or was she? As events dramatically unfolded it was discovered she wasn't in fact due to inherit anything!

The full story begins in the Wolverhampton area in 1884 when she was born and christened May Charlesworth. Her father worked as a mechanic in the developing field of engines and automobiles in Stafford. By 1900 when no more mention is made of him, her mother Miriam was living in Flowerburn House, Montrose, Scotland with her three daughters, and this is when the real intrigue begins.

It seems she had made it be known to a certain Dr. Barratt

that both May and her eldest daughter were due to inherit a staggering seventy five thousand pounds upon reaching their twenty first birthdays. On the strength of this expected windfall Miriam had borrowed substantial sums of money and obtained various goods on credit. Unfortunately the daughter whose name I have not been able to discover died at the age of nineteen. This left an embarrassed financial vacuum for all concerned. One furniture retailer actually took Miriam to court but bizarrely the judge found that the furniture store's recklessness in giving unsecured credit was a greater crime than Miriam's intentions, and the case was apparently dismissed!

It was around this time in Scotland that May, now eighteen re-named herself Violet and started putting it about that she was to receive a settlement of a hundred and fifty thousand pounds from an Alexander McDonald when she reached twenty five. It seems she learnt well from her mother as a pattern now appeared to be emerging!

Once again credit and monetary gifts were obtained which

The Minerva and possibly Miriam

apparently included a couple of cars and two leased houses; one over the border in England. By the time she was twenty one this façade may have been wearing a little thin because she suddenly declared that McDonald had left the country and was last heard of in Melbourne! Unsurprisingly it is now thought that he never actually existed.

By 1907 the Charlesworths thought it prudent to move so Miriam, Violet, her sister Eileen and their chauffeur moved down to Wales and took a house in the then fashionable Foryd area of Rhyl.

Now it was to be another doctor who would become Violet's main focus of attention, Dr. Edward Jones. And this time her story was that she stood to inherit a hundred thousand pounds from no lesser a person than Gordon of Khartoum; but not until her twenty fifth birthday. Having already inserted 'Gordon' as her middle name people were told that he had been her god father and following his heroic demise defending Khartoum in 1885 his will had made a generous provision for his god daughter when she came of age.

By now she apparently had a fleet of expensive cars and was always seen wearing a flamboyant red leather cloak whenever she was motoring! Violet was seen wherever it mattered and could mix with the best. It is easy to imagine her taking a drive along the empty roads up to the Denbigh Moor, perhaps to visit Lord Devonport's 'Gwylfa Hiraethog' shooting lodge which dominated the Hiraethog skyline and was a popular venue for dignitaries of the time.

She had an affectionate St. Bernard dog which apparently accompanied her everywhere. Another appendage to her image and was often worn was the diamond tiara she had been gifted by one of her many smitten admirers; her collection of 'gifted' jewellery was legend. She was the beautiful socialite to be seen with for anyone who was anyone; a femme fatale who must have cut a striking figure gracing and charming her way through the upper social circles of Northern Wales.

Boderw House, St. Asaph

They didn't stay very long in the Foryd, citing the noise of the trains as their reason for leaving. They took the impressive Boderw House in St. Asaph which is now the large hotel on the roundabout and many locals knew it as the place where she kept her St. Bernard.

Her eccentricity and flamboyance manifested itself in other ways; all no doubt contributing to her appeal. She wrote a song "Come back to Scotland" and sent it to both King Edward and the famous music hall comedian Sir Harry Lauder!

One could conjur up a plethora of adjectives to describe her obvious social skills which allowed her to penetrate even the stand offish and well established social defences of the Edwardian upper class.

By 1908 Violet was speculating heavily on the Stock Exchange using the money she had borrowed against her inheritance. Dr. Edward Jones had loaned her five thousand and a woman from Derby five hundred to name but two. By late Autumn she had lost twenty seven thousand pounds; a fortune today, but a massive amount in those days. She owed one notable London broker ten thousand pounds.

Had her speculations been successful there might not have been a story to write but they weren't and despite her charisma by winter 1908 Violet was in too deep a pit to climb out of.

When December arrived her debts were enormous (almost a million pounds in today's money) and her well documented 'inheritance' only a month away, things were closing in and she knew it. Violet would be twenty five on January 9th and her creditors had already made known their patience was running thin. What was she to do?

In the early hours of January 2nd Violet, her sister Eileen and their chauffeur (who has since been rumoured to have been her secret husband), were travelling east along the coast road above the sea cliffs of Penmaen-bach. It is unlikely we will ever know exactly what happened but, as mentioned, the car was found hanging over the wall with its windscreen broken. In all probability the accident was staged and Violet Charlesworth had disappeared.

Over the next few days several determined searches were made, finding only her hat and diary. Police, however were not convinced by this clumsy attempt to feign her death and a nationwide search was instigated. Her photo was placed in all the national newspapers as her shocked friends and creditors began to grasp the reality of the situation.

There were sightings in Worthing and even in Ireland. Several of these creditors even turned up at Boderw on her birthday in the vain hope that somehow her 'inheritance' would materialize and settle their debts!

A fortnight later a young journalist found her living under an assumed name in Oban; she had returned to her beloved Scotland much as the words of her song may have predicted.

Both she and her mother Miriam were convicted on February 21st of fraudulently obtaining several sums of money; one sample case involving borrowing four hundred pounds from a Martha Smith going back to 1903. They were both given five years 'hard labour' later reduced to three.

When they were released in February 1912 Violet and her mother disappeared for good this time and neither were ever heard of again.

Several historians have tried to discover where she went, who she became and how she lived but with no success. She vanished as mysteriously as she had lived her life, leaving more questions than answers.

Having done the research I too can't help wondering what became of her. She would still have been in her vivacious prime when she was released and the world would still have been her oyster.

Did she I wonder find that elusive formulae of obtaining money for nothing having learnt the hard way 'what didn't work'?

Perhaps she unleashed herself and her skills on the continent.

Or did she, as I like to think, meet someone who was a settling influence and eventually live a normal happy life somewhere in Scotland to bring up a family.

I can almost visualize her as an old lady in the swinging sixties occasionally thinking back to her 'other life', a twinkle in her eye, moist with sadness perhaps as she thought of a big slavering St. Bernards wagging its tail as it walked with its mistress in the grounds of Boderw.

She may, in her dotage have drifted off to sleep some nights dreaming of dashing along the empty lanes of Dyffryn Clwyd in her Minerva, her red cloak flapping in the wind.

During the Great War several of the Minervas were adapted as light attack vehicles against the Germans; would it be fanciful to speculate whether Violet's re-possessed pride and joy went down that route?

A criminal she certainly was but the flawed beauty who was Violet Charlesworth has managed to maintain an enigmatic mystique which has survived even to this day.

Chapter 14

Cornish "Morons"?

This comical little tale is loosely based on one of the many injustices imposed on the quarry workers of Bethesda by the tyrannical nineteenth century owner, Lord Penrhyn. In it, I disassemble what has become a folk memory, but whose roots lie in a confusion of facts, similar sounding words, and professional resentment.

It also shows how, by dropping a single letter a word can take on a completely different meaning, without any intention of malice. I also describe an amusing little trip which resulted as a result of hearing the story.

Deep beneath the quarry

The Bull – centre of the universe

"His uncle wasn't much better either, using morons from Cornwall to dig a tunnel when the local lads could have done a much better job!"

...was one of the tirades offered during an impromptu lecture I received in The Bull one evening. The Bull was the centre of the universe in Bethesda on a Saturday night, a few years ago. The assembled worthies, all at least sixth generation locals, had slipped comfortably into 'historical experts' mode and were gnawing away at their pet subject; maligning the second Lord Penrhyn's arrogant intransigence during the Great strike of 1904.

I continued to listen to this latest, new input with interest, as the narrator went on to describe the building of the quarry's main drainage adit in the 1840s by the said 'morons from Cornwall' in preference to local labour. I was intrigued, not just by the prospect of a tunnel to explore, but by the real story which obviously lay hidden beneath this bitter folk memory kept alive in the telling.

Even whilst I was listening I realized the word 'morons' was not intended as a derogatory insult to Cornish miners, but I certainly sensed a story lay hidden somewhere, in what was obviously a mistaken or changed word.

The result of my research cannot fail to make you smile, as I unravelled the real story to reveal a comical confusion of words, memories and even tunnels.

Following his heavy handed acquisition of numerous small quarries dotting the hillside above Bethesda in 1782, Richard Pennant was made Lord Penrhyn. In 1783 he began developing a quarry which was to become one of the largest in the world. By 1840 his Manager W. Francis realized that any further expansion would have to go down into the mountain. The palaeozoic mud which was compacted millions of years ago to form the Blue Penrhyn slate, was amongst the best in the world, and would justify the considerable expense of digging down into the mountain.

He sought advice from Robert Stephenson, who was at the time overseeing the building of the Britannia rail bridge over to Anglesey.

There were two problems with digging down. One, was having to raise the slate and the considerable waste material to ground level where it could be dressed. The second, and bigger problem would be the water. The quarry was a 130 acre site, and one night of rain would mean three million gallons of water with nowhere to go. It was agreed that a drainage tunnel would be necessary. The site chosen for its egress was near the little hamlet of Tanysgafell, two kilometres away where it could empty into the river Ogwen.

Initially things went reasonably well, but then a series of problems were encountered. The main difficulties were leakage and roof collapse at the point where the tunnel passed beneath a small lake called Llyn Meurig. The lake no longer exists; it lies buried beneath tons of slate waste dumped in subsequent years, but an old map of the quarry at the time clearly shows its

Tunnel entrance at quarry

Tunnel exit

presence. It seems the bed of the lake comprised of unstable blue clay. Each morning the men came to work to find a new section of tunnel had collapsed in the night. The problems, which lasted for almost a year were not only frustrating, but costly. Two project engineers came and went, and things slowly ground to a halt.

Eventually a new engineer was employed; George Twigge. His solution was to install 75 yards of iron arches along the section passing beneath the lake, but to do this he had to employ men who had experience of working with this method. He found these in Merthyr Tudful. Needless to say, employing outsiders went down like a dose of measles with the locals. In addition many of the Merthyr miners who moved up with their families were Mormons and this no doubt further upset the non-conformist, monogamous quarrymen of 'Pesda (Bethesda).

Inevitably, over many years of telling the story, and no doubt fed by this chagrin, the miners' religion was forgotten, and 'Mormons' became 'morons' as these imported tunnelers became the 'bad guys'.

But how did the Cornish element slip in? Well, it seems there are two other tunnels on either side of the river, about half a mile down from the drainage adit. These were in fact copper mines, which were apparently worked day and night between 1764 and 1770 by a group of Cornish miners, who kept themselves to themselves. They were managed by a Cornishman called Climo. A couple of us later explored these 'Cornish' tunnels, and although interesting, do not go in any further than 80 yards.

So this half remembered rail and gripe, sustained by anecdotes in naturally occurring social hubs like the Bull has, like 'chinese whispers' produced a memory whose link with the truth can only be described as comical!

And that was why, one Saturday morning, OD, Binks, Dash and I dressed in a variety of appropriate apparel, waterproofs and armed with torches set off for Tanysgafell tunnel.

The real Cornish tunnel

There were actually two entrances, the main one, and another which joined from the side a couple of hundred yards away. We opted for the main one, so we could claim a full length traverse.

The slow flowing water which was perhaps a foot deep, stretched from wall to wall and our hopes of a dry path alongside immediately evaporated. Bink's powerful torch which reached further than we could see confirmed it was going to be a wet trip. We lowered ourselves in off the bank and sank another foot into fine slate silt, making wellingtons totally useless. It became immediately apparent that this wading in cold evo-stik was going to be hard work. The first hundred yards brought some light entertainment as Binks took one step without his wellington! He was rewarded with an unsympathetic group laughter. Luckily he stayed upright as he got his foot back in. We passed the short side tunnel which offered the alternative entrance, and carried on to reach the section beneath the old lake. At one point a strange orangey-brown calcite growth tinged with rust had seeped from the roof which OD baptized the 'Devil's Hernia'. Another section sported what looked like an upside down ice cream cone, this, we duly named 'Penrhyn's phlegm'. Several mini stalactites and frozen tears adorned the tunnel roof as we steadily headed our way south towards the quarry. By now we had refined the most efficient way of walking; the trick was to stay still as each foot was pulled vertically and free of the suction, and then to move it slowly through the water so as not to cause too big a wave, before putting it down and repeating the process with the other foot.

The smack of waves hitting the walls, the slurp of feet pulling out of the glutinous mud, and their loud echoes made conversation difficult. Each time we stopped to examine or discuss something it allowed the reverberating sounds to die away making the settling silence quite a contrast.

We had been going perhaps twenty minutes when we came across an ancient broken floodgate; it had been totally smashed

Orange seepage

'Penrhyn's phlegm'

'Devil's Hernia'

by a force which we certainly wouldn't want to encounter. We pressed on, hoping the sudden flood which had destroyed it was just as ancient.

Shortly after this, some sections of the tunnel floor were raised, and soon we were able to walk on relatively dry sections. Our feet were heavy with clinging slate mud, much like a wet teaspoon which has been repeatedly put back in the sugar bowl.

Broken floodgate

We could feel a breeze at this stage, and sensed we weren't far from our objective, the main quarry. Then, up ahead, Dash noticed an eerie, pale light to our right. This turned out to be the foot of a 300 foot lift shaft. Its base was adorned with all sort of surprising rubbish, which included a twisted bike, a yellow safety helmet, a couple of crushed fifty gallon drums and some sheep bones, still in their wool. The sides of the shaft comprised of a latticework of timber, most still in situ, but many were rotten and on the point of collapse. The metal headframe at the top could be seen with a blue and white patch of sky high above.

Up ahead the tunnel opened out into a chamber, with another tunnel leading to one side. We decided to explore this one after reaching the main quarry entrance, which could only have been a hundred yards away. A huge pit yawned to one side with a massive pump, like a mechanical giraffe with its head in the ground. This was one of a pair used to draw the water from the lower levels of the quarry. This water would then be used as a cantilever weight to lift the slate and waste from the bowels, and eventually left to drain down the tunnel we had just traversed. Several giant tools lay abandoned on the side, including one spanner which would have fitted a dinner plate, Gulliver must have experienced something similar in the land of the giants! It was a melancholy sight to see engineering on such a scale locked in rust, and abandoned forever out of sight.

We had reached the 'Sebastopol' gallery and were mere yards from the tunnel entrance, where it opened out into the main quarry and the large blue lake; but where? We could feel the breeze coming through a huge pile of slate waste, and then, it suddenly hit us that it was blocking our way out, the tunnel was choked with roof debris; it was a disappointing blow. I knew from my reading, that the 'George' gallery was also on the same level, and connected to the drainage system so we decided to return past the big 'giraffe' pump and explore the other tunnel.

We set off along this new branch confident of reaching our goal, after all, the water was coming from somewhere! We had the vague idea of clambering out of the main quarry pit to return to Tanysgafell overland. We had gone perhaps thirty yards down this new tunnel when it became apparent that the water was significantly deeper, and the slate mud if anything stickier! When it reached our waist and a couple of us had nearly come to grief, the easy but reluctant decision to turn back was made, amid face saving declarations to return with inflatable kayaks to complete the trip. To say we were disappointed would be an understatement, but on the positive side, we had now discovered the source of the grey treacle we had been wallowing through for the best part of an hour.

Suddenly the cavern was filled with a bellowing roar, followed by a panicky higher pitched appeal from Binks, the heaviest and least mobile of our fellowship. He had been bringing up the rear of our retreat, and was well and truly stuck!

Lads being lads, the opportunity to practise some wit and one sided humour was enthusiastically embraced. One suggestion was coming back in the morning with some cheese sandwiches for him! Could he swim? OD was sure there was a dry pair of underpants somewhere in the car. To which one of us would he bequeath his expensive torch? We each offered a reason why it should be them. He was even asked for his next of kin! Eventually of course a couple of us supplied enough traction for him to come out with an almighty plop, whereupon he was slapped on the back and declared to be a boy.

Twenty minutes later we felt the warmth of the outside; wading with the flow back down the tunnel had been slightly easier.

Today, the quarry management have decided in their wisdom that to go any deeper is uneconomical, and the main pit has, consequently been allowed to flood. A large cobalt blue lake, which must be at least four hundred feet deep fills the lower quarry, right up to the level of the drainage tunnel, which is still doing its job. The tunnel mouth at Tanysgafell has a rusted grill bolted over its entrance, and the little side entry two hundred yards away has been blocked with builder's rubble. And although the quarry is still operational, albeit on a smaller scale, the dominant sights and sounds seen there today are the ever popular zip world rides, with their whirring electrical sounds as their passengers fly over the blue lake at 100mph.

When I shared my findings and description of the trip in the Bull some time later, the story of the trip through the tunnel went down well. But when I tried to explain the confusion over the Mormons/morons and the Cornwall connection, I was made to feel as If I'd just told a group of toddlers that Santa Claus wasn't real!

There was a brief silence before the old man at the corner of the bar cleared his throat, and said " Merthyr Mormons or Cornish morons, they weren't 'Pesda lads' who got to dig the tunnel were they?"

Chapter 15

The Crypt

In this chapter I describe a nocturnal 'jolly' I might have made some 36 Octobers ago. I say 'might' because technically the trip would have entailed trespassing and I certainly wouldn't want to admit to trespassing in print.

Chapel above the crypt

Dinorwig quarry

Just over a century ago the two largest slate quarries in the world ate into the opposite flanks of the same mountain in Snowdonia. The owners, both individuals, enjoyed vast, unimaginable wealth and power and lived in extravagant manorial homes not dissimilar to that depicted in Downton Abbey. The Pennant family of Penrhyn Castle had made their fortune in the sugar plantations with all the abhorrent slave connotations which came with it. They owned the quarry dominating Bethesda. Assheton-Smith lived in the thousand acre Faenol estate between Bangor and Caernarfon and his reputation fared little better. In 1806 he had forced a bill through parliament allowing himself to enclose over 2,500 acres of common land. When the locals protested he quelled the ensuing riots with cavalry! It was on this land he developed Dinorwig quarry above Llanberis. Not only did they own the quarries which provided work for over 5,000 men between them but they also owned most of the houses where the workers and their families lived; in 1900 Assheton-Smith owned 36,000 acres! Their power was absolute.

Nant cottage

An oft told tale relates how Nant cottage which is on the Caernarfon to Bangor road was in the way of the seven mile wall being built around the Faenol. The owner's reluctance to sell was met with a "Name your price" offer. The price asked for was for the amount of gold sovereigns it would take to cover the roof! Surprisingly, this was agreed but when the owner pointed out that he meant them to be on their edges the Agent acting for Assheton-Smith stormed off and the wall was duly built around the cottage. This was in 1863 and the cottage can still be seen today! Neither family were popular outside their own social class and there are deep rooted resentments over the many injustices they perpetrated still smouldering in the area today.

The agricultural depression which began in the 1870s, followed by the introduction of Death Duties in 1894 rang the knell for the landed gentry. Following the Great War, the ensuing social changes and the incremental increases in these inheritance taxes meant the days of the great estates were all but over. Dozens of farms, parcels of land and houses were auctioned into private hands during the middle years of last century. Dinorwig quarry closed in 1969 and in 1980 Sir Michael Duff the last of the Assheton–Smith dynasty died leaving the crumbling estate to a nephew who promptly sold it. Penrhyn quarry was sold to McAlpines in 1963 and the castle is now owned by the National Trust.

Loosely set within this context of class division and social oppression as a backdrop is the adventure I am about to relate!

It was during the early eighties shortly after Duff died and the Faenol estate was between ownership that I happened to be perusing the OS map of the area. I noticed a building marked 'mausoleum' in the middle of the woods on the estate; it looked interesting!

My ancestors would have had to curtsy or doff their caps in the presence of these privileged nobility when they ruled in all their opulent glory. Like hundreds of other families mine lived their hard, simple lives working for the estate and were buried in the local churchyard. Perhaps I thought, I should go and see what's so special about a landed gentry mausoleum.

Tentative enquiries through various pub based contacts in the area eventually indicated that access to a crypt beneath the mausoleum was possible through an underground tunnel. I was also warned to exercise extreme caution as the authorities were presently very touchy over trespass. By authorities I envisioned tweed capped gamekeepers sporting bushy sideboards and armed with shotguns. It seemed however there was also a security firm

Mausoleum and gate

employed to cover the smooth transfer of the estate.

Working on the premise that the further away our car was parked the less chance it would be linked to figures seen (and hopefully escaping) through the vast woodland if challenged, thus we prudently parked a good half hour's trek away! So, one dry but windy night three of us clad in black (but without any boxes of Milk Tray) slipped out of the car park of the Gardd Fon pub in Felinheli and started our two mile hike through the darkness. The moon was no wider than a clipped toenail hiding behind fast moving clouds as we left the village and approached the imposing boundary wall.

The first test was by-passing a lodge without alerting the usual barking dogs, fortunately the wind in the trees helped dampen any noise we made. This set the tone for the rest of the journey and hushed whispering was the only communication for the next half hour. We each had a torch but didn't use it, relying instead on our night vision, six saucer wide eyes straining to discern between different shades of black as we navigated with a luminous compass. About half way in we suddenly froze as a noise resembling a growling cat and a baby's cry came at us from above; it turned out to be two branches rubbing in the wind! A few minutes later a startled woodpigeon gave us as good as it got and set our hearts racing; proof, if it was needed just how tense we were! We were on 'orange alert' expecting the imagined legion of gamekeepers to leap out on us any moment! The leafy canopy above and the clouds between them ensured we rarely saw the moon as we slowly made our way through the woody labyrinth. A couple of tawny owls hooting somewhere in the canopy above accentuated the atmosphere appropriately. Every snapped twig, rustle of clothes or muted cough made us cringe as we slowly progressed through the restless trees. There are very few places above ground as dark as a forest at night.

Eventually we did glimpse the moon sailing through the scudding clouds and we realized we'd arrived at a small glade and must be near our target. Within seconds we spotted a darker shape rearing up out of the darkness and rusty iron railings draped with ivy and brambles. The mausoleum! It was everything I'd dreaded; a dilapidated gothic structure with high arched windows straight out of a Hollywood horror film, it lacked only giant bats erupting out of the belfry! We inched along looking for the massive slate slab said to be guarding the tunnel entrance using only one torch. The tunnel existed so workmen could access the crypt to do what workmen did in crypts without having to go through the family chapel above. A few moments later we found it; 'the portal to the tombs'. I immediately sensed a flicker of communal hesitation as the reality of where we were about to go hit home! Our 'macho' self images however prevailed, and we started to slide the slate across. It was heavy and the scraping sound seemed loud enough to wake the 'expecting dead' (or alert the gamekeepers!) but we were rewarded by the sight of iron rungs descending into the black depths.

A series of 'what ifs' hit us. 'What if our torches gave out?' 'What if someone replaces the slate and puts a rock on it?' 'What if there's something or someone down there?'

We slipped in like three nervous infants. Going first wasn't favourite but OD gamely took the lead, (it was after all his pub contact who'd told us about the tunnel!) Dash and I followed in that order. We gathered at the foot of the twelve foot ladder in an extremely low tunnel no higher than two foot; cramped together, lathered in sweat and tingling with adrenalin. We had to crawl on all fours for perhaps twenty yards until we emerged at the junction of two other tunnels in which we could stand. We chose to go right for thirty yards around another corner until we saw some steps ahead curving up to the left. At the same time a huge oak door adorned with 'treasure chest' hinges appeared on our left a few inches ajar; this had to be it. Never in our wildest dreams had we expected access to the actual inner sanctum where the late and great lay at rest!

Choosing to explore the stairs first seemed the obvious soft option to give our thoughts some time to digest this 'open door'. At the stair head a matching door was eventually 'persuaded' to open with a suitable creak into the musty abandoned chapel. A recess in the floor indicated where the coffins would have been lowered following the service to the waiting workmen below. The windows were high, too high to see through and were there only to provide light. A small bat appropriately flitted through the dust motes was caught in our torch beams as we read some sprayed graffiti on one of the walls, "Shaz woz ere". The unmistakable air of decay pervaded everywhere which was something more than rotting wood and crumbling plaster. A melancholy atmosphere echoing perhaps the only use this building ever had was for family funerals. Its very fabric seeped sadness.

We turned back down the stairs, with some reluctance it has to be said, the option to escape to the relative cheeriness of the forest, the way 'Shaz' must have come in was tempting! With much trepidation and still whispering we descended once again into the bowels wondering what awaited us beyond the oak door.

Through the gap our lights picked out a series of thick slate shelves containing coffins! The hinges squealed alarmingly as we tentatively pushed the door open. The vault we entered was about twenty feet long by twelve wide with alcoves on both sides. Some were bricked up, their tenants out of sight for ever, some contained coffins and some were empty waiting for members of a family which had become extinct! Then came the biggest shock of the evening! Up to that point we had diligently adhered to the roles of respectful visitors, interested, awed and without thoughts of malice. Suddenly we were staring at the result of mindless vandalism, an incursion many leagues beyond the innocent purpose of our expedition which was motivated only by curiosity and to merely 'not doff our caps!' We hadn't expected carpets, candles and incense but we certainly hadn't expected to see the wanton desecration we witnessed in that awful vault.

I felt very uncomfortable to be somehow sharing the label of 'trespassers' with the disrespectful perpetrators of what we saw. This grisly and degrading stripping of dignity was a rude demonstration that mortality was the ultimate equalizer and made me feel very humble.

We stayed three or four minutes, and in that time very little was said; there was very little that could be said. The incongruous presence of a crushed lager can adorning one 'shelf' was too offensive to leave behind; I took it with me. It was time to go, and the question of whether the slate lid at the end of the tunnel was as we had left it became a priority once again. We so wanted to get out.

This time we jockeyed positions not to be last; I lost, and as we crouched our way along the tunnel it was easy to imagine the ghost of Harris, my old high school headteacher, an arch enemy from twelve years before grabbing the nape of my neck! Entering the final low tunnel still as last man, my imagination went into overdrive as Harris mutated into the most nightmarish creature I tried not to imagine intent on dragging me back by my ankles!

Thankfully the exit was clear and there were no gangs of gamekeepers waiting for us. I've never climbed a ladder so fast! We quickly replaced the slate and vanished into the trees. There was a certain 'uncoiled spring' nonchalance in our gaits as we allowed the wind buffeted forest to swallow us in a healthier darkness than the one we'd just experienced with torch lights. The little compass became our friend once again as we headed back. We still kept quiet and paused to listen occasionally whenever the wind momentarily died but the relaxed tension was obvious and manifested itself in the odd whispered joke or ribald comment. We heard the same spooky rubbing of branches and we actually jogged past the lodge; who cares about barking dogs when you're on the outside of the estate and within sight of the street lights?

The walk back had seemed quicker and 200 yards from the

Sealed oak door

car conversation returned to normal decibels, as we began to process our experience and put it in some sort of order. We would sup a pint in our own 'local', seven miles away in Pentir, which by happy coincidence was called the Faenol Arms! There, the early versions of tomorrow's polished anecdotes would be born around the cheery bar fire.

Without a doubt it had been an adventure and the sights and emotions we'd shared would be with us a long time. Once the immediate and generic 'Wow Factor' memories had been shared, compared and digested we were inevitably left with our distilled private thoughts and impressions. Mine couldn't escape from the irony of how worthless pomp can be when there is no one left to sustain it. The fragile sanctum of the Assheton-

Smiths had degenerated into a grisly museum that only served to make a good case for cremation! Wouldn't they have been better off in the local churchyard at peace with their erstwhile estate workers than yearning for a Tutankhamun-esque eternity? Even his peace had only lasted 3,000 years!

A few weeks after our visit the slate lid to the underworld was finally locked in concrete as was the oak door and floor access from the chapel above. We had damaged nothing and broken no laws but we were still left with a feeling of discomfort from having been there.

Long overdue, that awful crypt and its occupants from another age has now been sealed forever.

Junction with the small tunnel

When I recently visited the site in daylight, taking advantage of new footpaths criss crossing the estate I found the mausoleum's abandonment utter. Many of the stained glass windows are broken and there was a missing panel in in the main door allowing entry into the old chapel. Several muddy footprints down in the crypt tunnels along with the usual discarded bottles and sweet wrappers testify to many visits. Thankfully the old oak door is still sealed as is the portal above. The rusty old railings surrounding the building are still padlocked but the slate lid lies broken in three pieces whilst the pit below has been filled in. I took my photos but realise they would never convey the atmosphere of my first visit.

I left, wondering how long this melancholic listed building would survive; rising as it does out of the encroaching forest like a forgotten Inca temple.

Chapter 16

The Lady Vanishes?

I wonder how many of us remember being enthralled as a child, by stories told by an established doyen of the family, and growing up believing the story to be true, down to the last embellished detail?

Rhodgeidiog reservoir

As a schoolboy, I was blessed with having several relatives living and farming on Anglesey. There were five farms in fact, and each one had its own unique appeal. One was a cluttered, unkempt cemetery of dead implements and dark ramshackle buildings, ideal for ratting where I honed my nocturnal hunting skills. At another, which resembled a deliberately set up 'Can you spot the dangers?' farm, I taught myself some valuable survival, and self-preservation skills over a period of twenty years in a laid back setting totally devoid of any Health and Safety considerations. How I emerged with all my fingers, limbs, and eyesight was a minor miracle.

But the farm which forms the starting point for this story was Glasgraig Fawr in the parish of Rhos-goch, which was owned by my Uncle 'Now'.

He was one of nine brothers in a clutch of thirteen, (Nain was pregnant for nine years – Ouch!) and he, like several of his brothers knew the art of story-telling, without allowing accuracy to ruin them.

Old buildings of Glasgraig Fawr

One of these tales he used to tell concerned a train crash, which happened on the section of track crossing his land, some three hundred yards from the farm itself. According to my Uncle 'Now', following the crash, the engine driver had managed to crawl to one of the buildings to die under a manger. Brrr! Inevitably; to a nine year old boy, the idea that these buildings were haunted was accepted without question.

As I grew older, the pinch of salt needed with each telling of the tale also grew. And over the years so too did the gaps between its telling, until one day, I decided to find out the veracity or otherwise of Uncle 'Now's story.

Bearing in mind the way the tale was told, implied that Uncle 'Now' himself had found the poor driver. It was therefore with some surprise I discovered that although the accident did indeed happen, it was over forty years before Uncle 'Now' was born! He certainly hadn't allowed accuracy to spoil his story!

The accident happened a good mile 'up' the line from Glasgraig Fawr; and it's a dramatic and tragic story which has a twist in the tail on a par with one of Agatha Christie's famous conundrums. According to my modest research, this is what happened.

It had been raining heavily all day and all night on the 28th November 1877, and the rivers and lakes of Anglesey were full to the brim. None more so than the seven acre reservoir used to supply water to Rhodgeidiog fulling mill, two miles from Glasgraig Fawr. The dam was of rudimentary earth and stone construction, on the young river Alaw, which at that point is a stream no wider than a couple of feet. A mile downstream the shallow valley closes in on itself to form a small gorge of perhaps two hundred yards length. A lofty thirty feet above this gorge, a short wooden bridge carried the railway across. Its wooden supports stood either side of the lazy stream, down on the enclosed valley floor.

That fateful morning the first train of the day from Llangefni to Amlwch, calling at Llangwyllog, Llanerchymedd and Rhos-goch had left with five people on board.

Rhodgeidiog fulling mill today

Sometime just before dawn the tired old dam at Rhodgeidiog, which was probably saturated: collapsed, releasing a torrent of water to roar down past the old mill. A brown tsunami which plucked everything in its path to create a soup of hedges, bushes, the odd sheep and a couple of footbridges, as it swept down the shallow valley towards the bridge a mile away. In less than a minute, the terrible deluge squeezed into the narrow gorge thus intensifying its bulldozing effect. When it slammed into the wooden supports of the bridge there could only be one outcome; and the whole structure was carried away leaving only the rails, and a few sleepers hanging over the void like a giant fish skeleton.

When the train arrived a little later there could only be one outcome then too, and it plunged over the side down into the brown, muddy gorge. The engine was pulling two coal tenders, a passenger carriage and the guard's van.

The driver that morning should have been Robert Williams,

The bridge today

Abandoned rails approaching the bridge

but he had overslept, and William Taylor had taken his place. Here, fate in its most fickle form demonstrated it could be both kind, and cruel. Taylor was pulled out of the wreckage four hours later still alive, but badly scalded and crushed. He was taken to the Blue Bell in Llanerchymedd where he died the following day, he was 32 years old. The young stoker, John Saunders from Bangor, was only 19 years old and he too was badly burnt but managed to reach Cae Mawr farm to raise the alarm. He died shortly after and is buried in Glanadda cemetery, Bangor. Edward Hughes the Guard, also managed to drag himself clear but in attempting to clamber over the wreckage to the bank became trapped, and had to wait to be rescued. He later died of his injuries. That particular day an inspector happened to be on the footplate, ironically to inspect the track; he was 46 year old John Davies from Gaerwen. Trapped beneath the hot engine, in the chaotic nightmare of twisted metal and mud on the stream bed, he was scalded to death; he left twelve children and a widow.

John Davies the Inspector

Put in perspective, within the scale of other railway accidents of the time; it was only a minor disaster. Cae Mawr bridge was re-built with stone and has been known ever since as 'Pont Damwain', ('Accident bridge'). The passenger service stopped in 1964 under the infamous 'Beeching' cuts and the rail track taken over by the pharmaceutical company Octel, based in Amlwch, and used to transport their chemical products. Since 1993 however, when the Amlwch company ceased trading, the track has been unused, the rails are orange with rust and their sun bleached sleepers slowly rotting underneath. Alder groves, brambles and farm fences, block much of the track and although there has been some talk of re-opening it as a tourist attraction or even creating a cycle track it's presently a 'wait and see' situation.

The Agatha Christie conundrum?
Well, that morning a lady had bought a ticket for that particular journey but hadn't actually picked it up from the ticket office. She was, however, seen boarding the train in Llangefni. Bizarrely, following the accident she was never found either on the train or anywhere in the vicinity. Her coat, bag, and one of her shoes, were all that was found at the scene of the accident! Of course she may have got off at Llanerchymedd, or Llangwyllog. And without a ticket to hand in there would be no record if she had. It could be of course that she never even got on the train. These two explanations have always been the most comfortable, but they do not explain the presence of her belongings at the ravine. Who was she? There is no record of a missing person matching her description. Did she I wonder, survive, and take the opportunity to escape what may have been an unhappy life to start anew elsewhere? Many do every year. Or was she swept away in the swollen stream, to be buried in a peaty grave under a newly formed bank of the Alaw? The amount of soil and detritus carried down in such a torrent would have been significant, and would certainly have altered much of the stream's topography. A mile below the bridge, the river turns west to flow in to the Alaw reservoir which was constructed in the 1960s; in 1877 it was a huge area of bog containing numerous deep pools, where a body could easily lie hidden. The chances are we will never know!

On a recent walk along the old line to photograph these sites, I had just triumphantly emerged out of a particularly aggressive scrum of brambles when I stood for a moment to gaze across at Glasgraig Fawr and reflect on my Uncle 'Now's version of the story. I couldn't help thinking that his invention of the 'haunting' was an awfully convenient reason for an inquisitive nine year old nephew to keep away from all the sharp and rusty farm implements kept in the buildings. Then I turned around and looked across at the Alaw reservoir, thought of the missing lady and wondered whether any night fishermen frequenting that particular shore had ever seen anything they couldn't explain; a restless apparition without a coat perhaps and only wearing one shoe!

Chapter 17

Nocturnal Misdemeanours

'Things that go bump in the night' is a term often used to explain the inexplicable. This chapter has a quick look at a themed set of such occurrences which have found their way into our folklore.

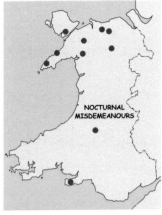

The old sign

Dinas Emrys

Whilst looking for something in the shed the other day, I came across an old wooden sign which immediately brought a smile across my face, and took me back some thirty five years. I had started to build a garage on a piece of land opposite a house I once owned. Initially things had gone well; the concrete base was solid and the strength and confidence of youth soon saw the breeze block walls coming along a treat. However, a couple of mornings later, following a windy night I awoke to find one almost completed wall had blown down. The lesson? I should have put a buttress half way along. The jibes from my friends came in thick and fast, references were made to Jericho, and several names for the garage, all referring to fallen walls were suggested. One friend even went as far as to make a sign – PARADFAIL! Parad being Welsh for wall! Quite clever! It was coming across this old sign which made me think of some of the many Welsh legends that have, as their main theme, walls collapsing overnight and masonry mysteriously moving. I thought I would share some of them in this chapter.

The most famous was King Vortigern's (Gwrtheyrn) attempts to raise a castle on Dinas Emrys, near Beddgelert in the fifth century. Having raised several hornet's nests in the south of England, which included betraying his fellow Britons, and losing the county of Kent to the Saxons, he had to flee to North Wales. Dinas Emrys is a dramatic looking hill with steep walls on all sides, and can be seen on the left of the A498 east of Beddgelert. Each morning when he and his builders arrived to continue working on the castle, the walls were found to have fallen during the night. This went on for several days before he consulted his wise men. Their considered advice was for him to find a fatherless, fair haired boy. The boy should then be sacrificed, and his blood spilt on the walls' foundations. Such a boy was duly found, and preparations for the grisly ritual were made. When the boy asked the reason for his death, and was told, he replied that the wise men were wrong. He went on to explain that beneath the hill there was a cave, and in the cave a lake where two dragons lived, one red and one white. Each night the dragons awoke to fight, and it was the tremors caused by these nightly fights which caused the walls to fall. That evening Gwrtheyrn sought the cave, and saw the wisdom of the boy's words. It was also that very evening that the red dragon managed to overcome the white one, and subsequently Gwrtheyrn was able to build his castle, the ruins of which can still be seen. Over centuries of telling, the red dragon has evolved to represent the ancient Britons, and the white one, the Saxons. The wise men were duly executed and buried in a field nearby, still called the 'Field of the Magician's Graves'. The young boy? Well, he was called Merlin, and he grew up to make a significant contribution of his own to folklore, especially of the Arthurian genre.

Although Denbigh has its own dragon legend, the dragon cannot be blamed for the unfortunate events which befell a new church which was built in the shadow of Denbigh Castle. The foundations were laid on St. David's day 1579 under the auspicious direction of the Bishop of Winchester. It was the Earl of Leicester's project, (Elizabeth I's favourite); and was intended to replace the Cathedral in St. Asaph. Each morning when the masons arrived to continue building, a significant portion of the walls had fallen and several stones removed. Work slowly ground to a halt, and eventually the intended church which was to be consecrated in St. David's name, became the far more modest St. Hilary's chapel. It is thought that the money intended for its full and grand completion was used for a military adventure in Ireland. Folklore, however, has a far more colourful explanation for its unattained potential. It would seem that a particularly active group of spirits did not wish the church to be built, and it was they who caused chaos during the hours of darkness. At one period it was used as a common barn, and was even a cock fighting pit. Today only the tower remains, and a flat piece of land where the once intended Cathedral and one time cock fighting arena once stood.

At one time there were two churches in Abergwesyn, a little village on the old drovers' road over the mountain between

St. Hilary, Denbigh

Site of the old church of Llanddewi, at Abergwesyn

Old Cemetery Llanfihangel Church, Abergwesyn

Tregaron and Llandovery. It was a strange arrangement to have two so close together on either side of the river Irfon which marked the parish boundary, but the explanation is even stranger. The original church in Abergwesyn was Llanddewi, but it was felt another church was needed for the neighbouring parish, and a site was chosen for the new church of St. Michael four miles away. Plans were drawn, and work commenced. However, on the second morning, when the workmen arrived the stones they had so painstakingly laid were missing. Word soon arrived that they had been found just across the river from Llanddewi church four miles away! When this happened for several days it was taken as a sign that St. Michael himself was choosing the site; and that explains how Abergwesyn had, at one time, two churches. One of Wales' famous Ministers and author Theophilus Evans had care of both churches in 1738, when he had the living of Llangammarch. Another notable Welshman, William Williams, Pantycelyn of hymn writing fame was curate of both churches in 1740. Both churches eventually fell to disrepair, and by the time Llanfihangel church was extensively re-built in 1871, financed by Miss Clara Thomas of Llwynmadoc, Llanddewi church was actually being used as a rough barn. Both churches were officially united in 1885. The new church however had to be demolished in 1964 because it had been built using poor quality sandstone; perhaps Abergwesyn was never meant to have a church?

There are only three churches in Wales, (if I discount Llanblodwel in the Tanat valley, just over the border despite its Welsh name), whose towers were built separately to the main building. St. David's cathedral, Llangyfelach, which is just north of Swansea and Henllan church just outside Denbigh. The furthest corners of the parish once reached fifteen miles away, and St. Sadwrn's church tower was built on a rocky hillock above, and some forty feet away from the church in Henllan so that the bells calling the faithful could be heard. But once again we have stories of the building material being moved mysteriously in the night to a spot much closer to the main church; uneasy spirits perhaps, or locals emboldened with spirits from the nearby tavern the 'Llindir', who didn't want a separate tower?

Today, many farms in holiday areas have diversified to become caravan sites, a sad indictment perhaps that more

Henllan church and separate tower

money can be made this way than through agriculture. Centuries ago, on the north coast of the Gower, there existed a small village called Llanelen. The church was dedicated to Helena, the roman wife of Maximus; he was the Emperor of Rome's Western Province around 388 AD. We know the village existed in 1319 because a document shows one Sir Robert De Penres paying a silver penny to rent seven acres of land belonging to the Norman Baron William De Breos. De Breos was famously hanged by Llywelyn the Great for his infidelity with Joan, Llywelyn's wife in 1230. But that is quite another story. Returning to Llanelen; one day a ship became grounded on the shore below the village, and it soon became apparent that all was not well. When the sailors staggered ashore the villagers realized that they were carrying the plague. As a result, many of the villagers died, and the survivors moved away, effectively abandoning the settlement for good. The little church too was left over the centuries to fall to the ground under the encroaching growth of grass, nettles and brambles. During a survey made in 1886 by J.D.Davies, a local historian, all that remained were the stones on the ground level of the church, a small patch which was the cemetery and an isolated Yew tree. Years later the farmer of Wern Halog, which is situated where the village used to be, decided to remove one of the old church's dressed stones for an intended purpose on the farm. That night he was kept awake by the noise of the stone being dragged across the farmyard. This went on for several nights, eventually, he decided to return the stone back to the ruined church. Several people have seen the apparition of a white lady in the vicinity of the old church; keeping an eye on the stones perhaps?

In a similar vein, the remains of another small church lies covered in growth, four miles to the north of Aberdaron on the Llyn peninsula. It was abandoned following the Reformation instigated by Henry VIII; because the worshippers had all been of the 'old faith'; catholic. Many years later the local farmer removed some of the stones and began work levelling the ground. That evening he fell ill, and very shortly afterwards died. The little church which is nothing more than a raised shape in the field, has been left alone ever since.

Yet another church, (what is it about these churches?) has a similar legend, although this one takes things a step further. When the village of Cynwyd near Corwen decided to build a church overlooking the Dee not only were the building materials moved in the night, but they went missing; never to be found. When this had happened a few times a wise man in the area came up with the solution that a white deer should be found, hunted, and wherever its blood was spilt when caught that should be the site of the new church. This was duly done, and the church was built on a raised spot about halfway between Corwen and Cynwyd. It is called Llangar church. The old church served this rural community for many years, standing about a mile downriver from Cynwyd. Ironically in 1856 it was felt a new church was needed nearer the village; this was subsequently built, and this time without any building materials vanishing. A

Remains of St. Meren

Llangar church

similar legend claims a white buck had to be hunted and killed before the church in Cerrigydrudion could be built. The original site of the intended church was 'Moel yr Eglwys' (Hill of the Church') over three and a half miles to the west. Today Llangar church has been in the safe hands of CADW since 1974 and a visit to see this well kept white-washed old building with its ancient stone graves is recommended.

This theme of sacrifice and blood pouring which is similar to the Dinas Emrys legend may be a mixture of pagan folk memory and old building practice. It is well documented for example, that Thomas Telford used blood from several hundred oxen as a constituent in the mortar used to build Froncysyllte aquaduct as recently as 1805.

Leaving the actual building work aside for a moment, there is an ancient unused church on Anglesey which has a curious singular stone. The ruins of the old church is today on private property, and the owners have addressed the issue of access prevention most enthusiastically with high walls and an electric gate. However I was able to visit a few decades ago and was smitten by the four ancient arches rising out of a carpet of wild garlic in May sunshine. There were two things of interest I was keen to see. The first came in the form of a small stoup built into the porch wall about four foot off the ground. No matter how dry the weather is, this little bowl is always full of fresh water and has neither a tap or pipe anywhere near it. It is thought some form of capillary action raises the water through the wall, which is probably built over a spring; most curious. The second thing I wanted to see, which has direct relevance to this chapter was a large stone, shaped like a man's thigh called 'Maen Morwydd'. Legend has it that the stone cannot be removed from the church. When Hugh Lupus, the Earl of Chester invaded Anglesey in his campaign against Gruffudd ap Cynan in the twelfth century he had his men drag the stone out of the church with chains, and threw it into the Menai Strait. Apparently, by the following night the 'Maen Morwydd' was back in the church, still wet and with fronds of seaweed clinging to it!

Moel yr Eglwys

Finally; one of the highest lakes above sea level in Wales is a little pool called 'Ffynnon Llyffant', high on the second highest peak in Snowdonia, Carnedd Llywelyn. The little cwm surrounding the lake is a jumble of glacial boulders. Folklore claims that one night in 1542 two of these boulders 'walked' the length of a bow shot away from the lake. It is also claimed that Henry VIII himself sent an envoy to discover the veracity of the tale and was assured the event had indeed happened!

These are just a handful of similar stories clinging to the theme of nocturnal moving rocks. I'm sure every district throughout Wales will have its own version of similar events, and I would be grateful if any reader does indeed have one he/she would be willing to share with me.

Chapter 18

Over the Migneint

Not somewhere that lends itself as a 'go to' location for tourists, this soggy plateau has definitely an acquired taste. The subtle attractions this bleak moorland offers, may be better enjoyed with a little appetizer describing some of the interesting features that can be found there.

The Migneint – remote but beautiful

One of my my favourite journeys by car, motorbike or bicycle is along the narrow umbilical tarmac which crosses the bleak plateau of the Migneint moors. The little road almost dares to venture over this wet upland. The Migneint is a desolate mixture of heather, rushes and rocks rising out of wet peat which forms a rough geographical triangle between Bala, Blaenau Ffestiniog and Pentrefoelas .Even on a hot August Saturday these moors retain their immunity from the hordes of ramblers

The last resident

who spread like a multi coloured fungus from the popular Snowdonian car parks most weekends. There are very few footpaths, even less 'stunning views' and a definite dearth of established cafes. Oh, and you would do well returning to the car with dry feet! But for those willing to read, search a little, and get wet there are several valuable pearls and interesting sites, which are well worth making the effort to visit.

On the highest point of the road from Ysbyty Ifan, is a junction with another little road which has climbed steadily from Penmachno. This too, is a narrow, tarmac intrusion into this upland snaking past the scenic little waterfalls of 'Ceunant Mawr' along the way. It was at this junction, a small tavern called 'Ty Newydd y Mynydd' once stood, along with four little

Sheep mural

cottages. A popular stopping off place for the drovers, the tavern which was last run by a character called Richards finally closed in 1893. It was occupied as a dwelling until the 1920s, but today, along with the cottages there is little to show that any of the buildings ever existed. There is however, a well on the site, which was renovated by Lord Penrhyn the then owner in 1846; and adorned with the words which translates as 'Drink and be grateful'. The well is known as 'Ffynnon Eidda'.

A mile to the south west the road passes the entrance to an old slate quarry which closed over a century ago. 'Croes y Ddwy Afon' quarry did re-open for a brief period in the 1980s, but has once again been abandoned. Opposite the entrance, which is now washed away by the stream, is a small lake nestling in a saucer like hollow. This is 'Llyn Dubach y Bont', and it is the traditional lake where the local fishing club, 'Cymdeithas Genweirio'r Cambria' place the little trout hatchlings to acclimatise, before being released into 'Llynnau'r Gamallt' and other high mountain lakes nearby. 'Llyn Dubach y Bont' is one of two similarly named lakes in Eryri. Half a mile to the west is another lake, 'Llyn y Morynion', another of the society's lakes. Here, according to the ancient stories of the 'Mabinogion', Blodeuwedd's maid servants fell headlong in and drowned whilst trying to escape Lleu's vengeance; it is a tale worth seeking out to read, and is one of Europe's oldest written stories. Another legend claims that it was here on this lofty spot that the men of Dyffryn Clwyd caught up with the men of Ardudwy who had conducted a raid and taken their womenfolk. A battle ensued, which was won by the Clwydians; but so enamoured were the women with their new Ardudwy men they threw themselves into the lake rather than return. It was on the shores of this lake in an eisteddfod held in 1906 that Ellis Evans first adopted the bardic name of Hedd wyn. He famously, and tragically won the 1917 National Eisteddfod Chair a couple of weeks after being killed in the Great War. The next road junction sports a small café which is occasionally open, there was a petrol station here for many years, but has by now, been closed for some three decades. The road left (east) will take you past the Celyn reservoir, and eventually Bala; whilst turning right (west) will lead down to Blaenau Ffestinog high above the dramatic gorge of 'Rhaeadr y Cwm'.

Rhaeadr y Cwm

Cefn Garw

We will now return to 'Ffynnon Eidda' at 1,576 feet above sea level and continue for another half a mile, until we reach a small bridge, with a parking space for one car on the right hand side of the road. From here, a faint footpath called 'Y Llwybr Coch' (the red path) will take us to one of the loneliest farmhouses in Wales, 'Cefn Garw'. Initially the tell tale tracks of a quad will show the steep trampled way, but upon reaching the remnants of a low wall the path becomes faint and veers to the left, before snaking its way back right. The path is easy to lose, but worth persevering to find the easiest walking. A significant outcrop of boulders and bedrock can soon be seen over to the right, these are called 'Creigiau'r Lladron', (Robber's Rocks). It was here, according to hearsay that Maredydd ap Ifan and his soldiers came upon a group of bandits hiding amongst the rocks. They had been plaguing the area in much the same way as the infamous brigands of Mallwyd. Like many such bands, they were possibly ex-soldiers from one of the medieval wars Britain was embroiled in, veterans, who could find no employment in peace time. It has even been suggested they were remnants of Glyndŵr's army. Maredydd and his men wasted no time in putting them to death; and buried them in the peaty bog nearby. He had moved away from 'Gesail Gyfarch', Eifionydd, to escape a family dispute, and lived for a period in Dolwyddelan Castle. His descendants went on to establish the Wynne dynasty of Gwydir Castle, Llanrwst.

Another cluster of rock, as we continue walking (or wading), south rears out of the marsh with a much graffitied border stone on its summit; these are 'Cerrig Llwynogod' (Foxes' rocks). Several have made their den here over the years, and the spot was a prime target for many organised hunts. Our way ahead continues, through drifts of heather, and clumps of rushes over undulating ground and several bogs. We crest a small rise almost half way to our goal, before dropping down to pass within three hundred metres of a small lake called 'Llyn Serw'. This lies in a large, wet bowl surrounded by a very marshy fringe. It was once full of hungry little brown trout, managed and fished by the Penrhyn estate but, as with many of these upland waters, decades of acid rain has alarmingly diminished the number of fish,. Andrew Foster who was the Head Gamekeeper for the estate kept a detailed diary of all his gamekeeping activities, and on the 4th October 1886 he records that 122 trout were caught to provide new stock for the Cambridge Angling Society. Four years previously two poachers had been caught by the lake and taken to Foster to be dealt with. One can only imaging the nature of the punishment he meted out!

It is a harsh environment up here, and although a few white quartz stones along the path are there to show the way, snow and mist would make this walk a serious undertaking. According to Nerys Ellis, Hafod Ifan whose family have leased this land for generations, it was the custom to turn these quartz rocks over every so often, to keep them clean and visible.

In less than an hour a final climb takes the path up on to another small hill sporting an incomplete wall, and there, the chimney of Cefn Garw can just about be seen, almost hiding in the shallow valley below. This wall, may represent the one time ownership of Cefn Garw and fifty acres of the surrounding valley by the monks of Aberconwy. It is also a good place to take

The Boy's Cairn

in the vista. Ahead, and beyond the old farmhouse is the river Serw, which drains this upland valley and contributes significantly to the waters of the Conwy, which it joins some three miles lower down. The rough slopes rising beyond, climb gradually to form the mountain Arenig Fach. Binoculars will reveal a cairn on the summit which has a sad story. It is called 'Carnedd y Bachgen' (the Boy's Cairn), and was built to remember nine year old Dafydd from 'Weirglodd Ddu' who was shepherding 'Cae Gwernog' sheep on Arenig's slopes. At some point, Dafydd became lost in the mist, and must have reasoned that his best chance of being found was on the summit. Unfortunately it wasn't until the following morning that he was found, he had died of hypothermia, and the poor little soul had wrapped his bare feet in his cap to keep them warm. A little below the summit, on the western side is a small shepherd's shelter which is only big enough for one man and his dog. It is said that the last to use it was John Thomas the famous ballad singer who partnered Bob Tai'r Felin' in various concerts around the country.

Ahead, a short mile to the south on the slope, rising from

the Serw is a pile of stones known as 'Cerrig y Bala'. This pile was left here when a giantess's apron strings broke. When one considers how many of these are found throughout Wales one wonders at the poor quality of these giantess's aprons. A little further west is 'Carnedd Iago', a small hill which marks the meeting place of the old boundaries of three counties, Caernarfon, Denbigh and Meirioneth. It was claimed that wrongdoers could claim sanctuary within the triangle formed by the three rocks on the summit. Today it is a disorderly arrangement of a rusty fence and loose boulders. The modern county boundaries meet a mile to the north west, and is marked by an impressive toblerone shaped rock containing the name of the three counties. Ednyfed Fychan reputedly fought a battle on the slopes of Carnedd Iago in his youth. He later became Llywelyn the Great's Chief Minister. And beyond Arenig Fach, almost as if it's trying to hide behind its smaller neighbour is Arenig Fawr, rising dramatically from the unseen shores of Llyn Celyn. Its complicated slopes still hide a casket of love letters, secreted by the artist James Innes, who was spurned by his lover,

Shepherd's Hut

Euphemia Lamb in 1911. He, and fellow artist Augustus John had rented Nant Ddu cottage at the foot of the Arenig Fawr for two years from 1910, during which time he became obsessed with the mountain. There are numerous paintings of his work still to be seen in various exhibitions. Sadly he was to die of TB in 1913.

Immediately below, and down the valley to the left we can see the long farm track which serves the old house of Cefn Garw, running parallel with the river. The track crosses the river with a ford some two and a half miles down. Probably the longest track to a dwelling in Wales, it wasn't until the 1980s that it was improved enough to be land-rover friendly. The valley is a quiet peaceful place with only the distant bleat of sheep, the odd croak of a raven, and the musical tinkle of thousands of little rivulets percolating their way through the peat down to the Serw. These are the only sounds to accompany the soughing of the wind. Every shade of green, brown and orange that is possible grows out of the wet black peat which blankets this hidden glen.

Somewhere on this broad watershed ridge which divides the Conwy and the Serw is a hidden cave. A passing harpist was once enticed inside by the 'Tylwyth Teg' (Little Folk); and never found his way out. Sometimes, when there's no wind whispering through the rushes, and you sit to listen in the right place, you can faintly hear his sad notes coming from deep in the ground.

The walk down to the house takes ten minutes. Cefn Garw has not been a dwelling for many years, the last person to live there was an old shepherd who worked for Hafod Ifan in the 1920s. It is not however, a ruin. Its roof is in a remarkable state of repair, as is its single outbuilding. When the Penrhyn estate owned Cefn Garw, it was used to provide sustenance for the aristocrats when they came up to shoot grouse under Andrew Foster's direction. On one day alone in the 1890s, his diary records 120 pairs were killed; no doubt a lot of caviar and brandy was also consumed; not a good era to be a grouse. The only entrance into the house is surprisingly and, refreshingly unlocked, but is quaintly held shut with a piece of rope. This is not the only surprise because when you walk in you are immediately confronted with a baby grand piano, adorned with a candle stick and a sheep's skull! It used to be pink, and only a few of its keys now work. The next thing one notices, is the large mural of a sheep on one wall. It is a mystery how either feature came to be there; the piano is a fairly recent addition, but the mural has certainly been there many decades. When one's eyes are adjusted to the gloom one is struck by how many people have signed their names on the wall. Most of these are local Welsh speakers who have been for a walk, or have popped in whilst working in the valley. Some record their reason for coming, many have visited as part of their work. It is worth recording a few :-

One of Hafod Ifan's workers, D.G. Jones came up on the same day (June 23rd) for three years running 1958, 1959, and 1960 to dam the river so the sheep could be washed.

Nerys Ellis herself wrote that four attempts to shear the sheep had failed because of heavy rain on 17 – 7 – 93

On 1st July 1979 the workers inside were having a break from shearing, when one of the lambs escaped and came running into the house!

July 6th 1990 shearing started at 8:30am and finished at 1:00pm and it is recorded that a huge fire was made in the old grate.

There is a note recording that Kelv, Will, Dick, Bee, and Salt had been up to repair dry stone walls on 5-6-98

Half a century after the National Trust bought the mountain in the 1950s there came a different emphasis on the work done. From 2010, there has been a move towards returning the habitat to its natural state, and some of the writings reflect this:-

Wins and John Bryniog came to close some ditches, March 2010. Many of the old timers would surely have turned in their graves, when they had worked so hard to open the ditches in an effort to drain the vast bog to make farming possible.

There are several references to hunting foxes, as well as fishing. But even as far back as 1957, the effect of acid rain on the fish population could be felt.

M.S.Owen fished Serw lake August 1957 but didn't catch anything.

Ken and Merrina also fished the lake 23-5-07, but no mention is made of any fish caught.

Ysbyty Ifan school children came for a walk 5-7-94

Prys called by on his bike on his way up Arenig Fach 7-9-06. When I consider the severity of the terrain I wonder if he made it.

More recently Rhodri Owen came looking for inspiration in the middle of the pandemic.

There are also snippets of poetry written on the walls and cupboards, many of these writings are in a poor state due to the damp crumbling plaster. I walked the 'llwybr coch' with my brother in 2021 and recorded as many of these scribbled writings as we could decipher. Interestingly enough over 90% of these messages are written in Welsh, the few examples above have obviously been translated.

The last shearing in Cefn Garw took place in 1999, but many of the old cups and plates used to feed the workers have survived in a wooden cupboard. Outside, the sheep dipping compound and collecting yard is a study of melancholy abandonment, best imaged perhaps by a metal pail hanging on a fence post above a rusty churn lying half covered in the encroaching rushes. Nettles and thistles grow freely in old sheep droppings where once there was so much activity. An interesting kennel type feature in one of the walls was used to contain any sheep-dog bitch on heat. It would be kept in this kennel and blocked in by a huge boulder; contraception, Migneint style!

Before leaving the loneliest farmhouse in Wales, duly secured of course with the rope, it is interesting to note that one scene from the film 'The Corn is Green' was filmed here in 1978. The path back to the car is a repeat of the approach, and due attention is needed to stay on the 'llwybr coch'; the alternative is uncomfortable wading through clumps of rushes, coarse lumpy grass and deep drifts of heather, and, depending on the weather, considerable wetness.

Back on the road, and half a mile towards Ysbyty Ifan is 'Pont ar Gonwy', the first bridge to cross one of North Wales's most significant rivers. It is a simple lintel bridge with three portals for the growing stream to flow through. The river then takes a sharp turn to the east to form a lively little waterfall cascading its cream and orange foam past a rock rising above its right bank called 'Y Garreg Ddefod'. The old shepherds would apparently call by this rock and offer a prayer before venturing up into the mountains. On the opposite bank to 'Y Garreg Ddefod', high above the river is the remains of the small dwelling, 'Ty Bach Pennant' with its peculiar pipe chimney. This is where the shearers using the outbuilding of the cottage on the road above would be fed by 'Aunty Nesta' from Hafod Ifan. The cottage by the road marked on the OS as Llyn Cottage was used by the Penrhyn family and their guests for many years. The housekeeper during the Edwardian period was called Anna Jane, and she live down in Penmachno, walking up whenever she had duties to perform. One evening during a particularly bad snow storm when she didn't turn up nothing sinister was thought to have happened because in such conditions she wasn't expected.

However, a thousand feet lower down in Penmachno, there had been no snow when she set off, consequently her family didn't expect her to encounter any difficulties. She was found the following morning, less than a hundred yards from Llyn Cottage, and had died of exposure.

The 'gate opening tramp'

Back at the car and on the road which was actually built by Lord Penrhyn in the nineteenth century (one of his more altruistic projects), and we head towards Ysbyty Ifan once again. In about a mile we reach a cattle grid, which replaced a gate which was here for many years. For a few summers following the second world war, a tramp used to come to this lonely spot and build himself a small turf abode beside the gate. Then, when a vehicle came, he would wander out, open the gate and hold out his hand; he was seldom refused a penny or two.

Just before reaching the village of Ysbyty Ifan a steep track climbs up on the left to Hafod Ifan farm, and then continues to Blaen Eidda bridge. This is a remarkably robust bridge considering the sparse population in this lonely upland. Here the road divides; the northern branch continues to eventually drop down to the A5, whilst for the western branch the tarmac ends. It continues as a very ancient, rough track which connected the settlements of Ysbyty Ifan and Penmachno, I have cycled this way many times. It is called 'Y Lon Llech' ('Slate Road'). It was somewhere along this old track that Richard

Powell died in a snow storm whilst walking over from Penmachno. He was a young man and kept the school in Ysbyty Ifan, he was also a fine poet who had won the Chair in the Bala Eisteddfod of 1793. Another, smaller bridge appears in a quarter of a mile, this is called 'Pont Rhyd yr Halen'. If one continues up the track for perhaps a hundred yards, and then walk some fifty paces in to the left of the track there is a lone boulder lying amid clumps of gorse. This was once used in weight lifting contests between local youths from both parishes, and is called a 'Carreg Orchest'. It is inscribed, but difficult to read. There are several of these around Wales, one outside the council office in Penmaenmawr, and another in the church in Llanwddyn to name but two. The little stream which flows beneath 'Pont Rhyd yr Halen' bridge has its source in a very wet area a mile to the south west. Perched just above this source is a very singular cube shaped boulder. This is 'Gwely'r Lleidr' (Robber's Bed), and is the traditional resting place of a notorious thief who troubled this area many years ago. It is said that whilst he rested on top of the boulder, his dog would lie at its foot and warn him

Weight lifting boulder

The Robber's Bed

if anyone approached. Apparently, one night, the dog died and the thief was caught asleep on his boulder.

The hill above is called Foel Boeth, and has on its flattish summit a little lake bearing several names, 'Llyn Brain Gwynion' (White Crows lake),'Llyn Talcen Llwyd' (Grey Facet lake), 'Llyn Bwlch y Gwynt' (Windy Gap lake) as well as LLyn Foel Boeth itself. If one looks at the 1:25,000 OS map one will see the parish boundary runs straight across the middle of the lake. In the old days it was an annual tradition for certain officers to walk the parish boundary, but when they arrived at this little lake it was considered sufficient to throw a stone across.

And that's a brief synopsis of the Migneint, enough perhaps to tempt a little more interest in this wet upland, whose composition constitutes coarse grass, rushes, heather and rocks rising out of black peat; and to demonstrate, that there is more here than a thin strip of tarmac threading its way through a soggy moorland.